Colin Chapman

CHRISTIANITY ON TRIAL

BOOK ONE

How can we know if Christianity is true?

Lion Publishing

EXPLANATION OF SYMBOLS

 Introducing each of the seven questions dealt with in the three books

 A road intersection sign then shows the various possible answers

 Each answer is then introduced by this route sign

Two further symbols appear within the answer sections:

 A one-way sign points out the effect or consequences of a particular answer

 A hazard sign shows the problems or questions arising out of the answer

LION PUBLISHING,
121 High St, Berkhamsted, Herts

First edition November 1972
Reprinted April 1975
ISBN 0 85648 007 X
Copyright © 1972 Lion Publishing

Printed in Great Britain by Compton Printing Ltd., Aylesbury

CONTENTS

ILLUSTRATIONS

Acknowledgements
British Broadcasting Corporation, picture on page 58;
British Museum, pages 16, 33; *Camera Press*, pages 21, 24, 25, 27, 32, 37, 67, 75, 87; *Hamish Hamilton*, page 44 (from *Vintage Thurber*, 1963); *National Portrait Gallery*, page 52.

GENERAL INTRODUCTION

'I could tell you my adventures – beginning from this morning,' said Alice a little timidly: 'but it's no use going back to yesterday, because I was a different person then.'

'Explain all that,' said the Mock Turtle.

'No, no! The adventures first,' said the Gryphon in an impatient tone: 'explanations take such a dreadful time.'

Explanations take such a dreadful time. But if we omit them, we are likely to meet with this reaction:

'What *is* the use of repeating all that stuff,' the Mock Turtle interrupted, 'if you don't explain it as you go on? It's by far the most confusing thing *I* ever heard!'

Is Christianity *true* or is it not?

How can we possibly *know* whether it is true or not?

These are the basic questions before us in putting Christianity on trial. We are dealing primarily with Christian beliefs about God and Jesus Christ, about man and the universe. We are asking whether they tell us 'the truth' about ourselves and about the universe in which we live.

But how can Christian beliefs be put on trial?

Questions about Jesus Christ

There was a time when it seemed very simple to prove the truth of Christianity. A Christian could stage a trial which ended like this:

Judge: Gentlemen of the Jury, I have laid before you the Substance of what has been said on both Sides. You are now to consider of it, and give your Verdict.

Foreman: My Lord, we are ready to give our Verdict.

Judge: Are you all agreed?

Jury: Yes.

Judge: Who shall speak for you?

Jury: Our Foreman.
Judge: What say you? Are the Apostles guilty of giving false Evidence in the Case of the Resurrection of Jesus, or not guilty?
Foreman: Not guilty.

This happened in England in 1729.

Recently a similar trial was staged in a youth club in Scotland, but with significant differences. This time a Christian was put on trial, and the charges against him were these:
1. that your faith is based on a myth – the resurrection;
2. that your faith is irrelevant to life in the twentieth century.
All who took part in this trial were speaking for themselves and expressing their own beliefs; they were not acting a part. A few were Christians, but most were not. The audience were the jury, but there was no vote at the end. The judge in his summing up simply explained that each person must decide for himself whether or not he thought the Christian was guilty on these two charges.

If the idea of this second trial appeals to you, or at least makes some sense to you, you may want to go straight to the third book in this series, which deals with the evidence for Jesus Christ, the meaning of his death and the question of his resurrection.

Questions about God, man and the universe

To many, however, this second trial will sound just as strange or absurd as the first. If you cannot understand or accept Christian beliefs about Jesus, it may be because you do not accept some of the most fundamental Christian assumptions about God and man and the universe, and not simply because you are not convinced by the evidence about Jesus.

Bishop Butler, writing in 1736:

It has come, I know not how, to be taken for granted, by many persons, that Christianity is not so much a subject for enquiry but that it is, now at length, discovered to be fictitious. And accordingly they treat it as if in the present age this were an agreed point among all people of discernment, and nothing remained, but to set it up as a principal subject of mirth and ridicule, as it were by way of reprisals, for its having so long interrupted the pleasures of the world.

J. S. Mill:

I am ... one of the very few examples, in this country, of one who has not thrown off religious belief, but never had it: I grew up in a negative state with regard to it. I looked upon the modern exactly as I did upon the ancient religion, as something which in no way concerned me.

Nietzsche, writing in 1865 at the age of 21:

If Christianity means belief in a historical person or event, I have nothing to do with it. But if it means the need for salvation, then I can treasure it.

Mahatma Ghandi:

I may say that I have never been interested in an historical Jesus. I should not care if it was proved by someone that the man called Jesus never lived, and that what was narrated in the Gospels was a figment of the writer's imagination. For the Sermon on the Mount would still be true for me.

Colin Wilson:

The need for God I could understand, and the need for religion; I could even sympathize with the devotees like Suso or St. Francis, who weave fantasies around the Cross, the nails and all the other traditional symbols. But ultimately I could not accept the need for redemption by a Saviour. To pin down the idea of salvation to one point in time seemed to me a naive kind of anthropomorphism.

If, therefore, your questions and objections about Christianity are about fundamental assumptions about God, man and the universe, there will be little point in making Jesus the starting-point of the discussion. You ought to begin with one or more of the questions in the second book in this series. Who or what is 'God'? Does 'he' exist? What is man? Who am I? What kind of universe do we live in?

Questions about definition and truth

But what if you are not sure what Christianity is?

James Mitchell:

I used to be a convinced Christian: I am no longer a convinced Christian: I am no longer convinced. In fact like many others of my generation I am profoundly uncertain as to what 'being a Christian' actually means any more.

C. E. M. Joad:

If you will forgive me for mixing my metaphors, to criticize Christianity is like assaulting a feather bed with the consistency of a jelly and the colours of a chameleon.

And what if the idea of putting *any* ideas or beliefs on trial sounds absurd?

The hero in Henri Barbusse's novel L'Enfer:

As to philosophical discussions, they seem to me altogether meaningless. *Nothing can be tested, nothing verified.* Truth – what do they mean by it?

Michael Harrington:

The contemporary spiritual crisis is the result of this simultaneous loss of faith and anti-faith ... Its unique characteristic is that no one really seems to believe in anything.

C. E. M. Joad writing about the war of 1914–18:

Then came the war ... When it came to the point, the ethics of Christianity were, it seemed, as incapable of practical application as its history and biology of scientific verification. The whole religion as it is taught and preached today thus came to seem a gigantic swindle ...

Margaret Cole:

It is partly because I care for verification that I cannot believe in any 'revealed religion' ... When the question of the *truth* of Christianity was raised in my mind ... I perceived almost immediately that it was not true, and that it could not possibly be proved to be true; and the burden of religious belief fell from my back as easily as did the burden of Christian in *The Pilgrim's Progress*, and has never shown any sign of returning to its perch.

If you share these feelings, or have a strong sympathy with those who feel this way, you will probably have to begin with the questions about definition and truth in the first book in this series.

The method and material used

Each of the main sections (in the case of Book One, the whole book) has an introduction outlining the general approach and defining the question being tackled.

Then the 'road intersection' shows the possible answers to the question.

Each answer is then examined in detail.

Much of the book consists of quotations from different writers, because it is important that we should try to feel the full force of what they are saying. Where there is merely a summary of a person's position, the summary is in most cases taken from a writer who has no particular axe to grind or does not share the outlook of this book (for this reason much use has been made of, for example, Paul Hazard's books *The European Mind 1680–1715* and *European Thought in the Eighteenth Century*). Where italics have been used they are the italics of the original author.

Quotations have been chosen from the philosophers, tracing the history and progression of their thought; from the arts, because often this is the area where beliefs can be worked out and carried to their logical conclusions; from other religions, because East and West are becoming more aware of each other's ways of thinking and no approach to Christianity should leave them out of account; and from modern theology which has been profoundly affected by the history of ideas.

Finally, some problems and questions about the Christian answers are dealt with.

The starting-point

What is 'Christianity'? There are so many definitions that it is necessary, before we begin, to say something about the starting-point of this book.

There are three possible ways of answering the question:

Try to find the lowest common denominator in all the different definitions of Christianity that are offered; limit the definition to include only those items which all Christians or the vast majority of Christians would accept without question.

Refuse to define Christianity at all. Allow each person to have his own understanding of Christianity, and show the maximum tolerance towards anything which is described as 'Christian'.

State your own understanding of what Christianity is, at least as a starting-point; further discussion will show to what **extent** it is consistent with the mind of Christ.

This third approach is the one I have adopted. I shall take as my starting-point what is generally called Biblical Christianity; *i.e.* dependent solely on what we know of God and Christ from the basic documents of the Bible, both Old and New Testaments. This understanding of Christianity is not that of any one church or denomination.

No discussion is held from a purely 'neutral' position. Therefore the aim in stating my own position is not to be sectarian and doctrinaire, but simply to declare the book's starting-point openly and clearly.

The position of this book, then, is basically a committed one. But its method is open. It is for the reader to start where he will, at the point where he is. He can examine the options, follow up which he wants in the order he wants. It may mean going back to an earlier question to be settled first.

Then it is for the reader to make up his own mind, to follow up the evidence – and act accordingly.

INTRODUCTION TO BOOK ONE

"How can we know if Christianity is true?"

The question is not: Does Christianity contain *truths*? Does it contain individual truths which can be combined with truths from other religions and philosophies?

The question is rather: Is Christianity itself *the truth*? Is the whole system of Christian beliefs consistent within itself, and consistent with everything else that we know? Do Christian beliefs, when taken together as a whole, teach 'the truth' about man, the universe and God?

The question is not simply: How can I know if Christianity is true *for me*? Is it true to my experience, true to my own understanding of myself (regardless of whether or not it expresses the truth about all men)? Is it true 'existentially'? Does it express the existential truth of my own experience (whether or not it is true objectively)?

The question is rather: Is Christianity objectively true? Does it give a true account of what is there? Is it true objectively *and* true existentially at the same time? Can it be true in my own experience simply because it is the truth about the way things are?

Many (if not most) people today have already concluded that Christianity cannot be true in this sense, or that it is impossible to know for certain. But we must ask the question in its simplest and most direct form. Is Christianity true or is it not? Is it true or false, or partly true and partly false? Or what . . . ?

The moment we put the question in this way, we are involved in the more fundamental question of how we can 'know' anything – the ways of knowing. Broadly speaking we may say that there are six different approaches to knowledge and belief:

The way of verification. We observe certain things through our senses, and we assume that they give us reliable knowledge about what is there. We then draw certain conclusions about what we perceive. Where we can, we carry out certain tests to eliminate false or inadequate theories, and to find the best and most convincing way of accounting for all that we observe.

The way of authority. We accept someone else's authority – the authority of an individual, or of a group, or of a consensus, or of a tradition. For example, most of what we believe about science is accepted on the authority of others, since we are not in a position to carry out the tests ourselves.

The way of abstract reasoning. We start with certain assumptions in our minds, and then demonstrate that once we accept these assumptions, certain things must necessarily follow and be true.

The way of agnosticism. Many reach the point at which they say that the other ways of knowing do not give us certain or even adequate knowledge. We must simply accept the fact that we do not know, and cannot know anything for certain. There are no fool-proof ways of knowing.

The way of intuition or blind faith. We believe certain things because we 'feel' that they are true. We cannot give rational arguments for them, but deep down we feel that they must be true. And sometimes we believe *against* the evidence; we find that there are good reasons for *not* believing, and yet we believe in spite of this. In this case we believe by a leap of blind faith.

The way of mysticism. This way, it is claimed, gives us direct and immediate knowledge of what the universe is all about. It can be acquired in many different ways, but it cannot be communicated adequately in words.

These six different approaches correspond roughly to the six basic answers which have been given about the truth of Christianity. These are set out as possible ways, or routes that can be taken, in the picture opposite. Some people combine elements from several of the answers. But it is necessary and helpful to try to distinguish them.

Choose the one that appeals to you most. Then turn to the page shown: see whether the answer satisfies you or whether you then want to turn to one of the others.

How can we know if Christianity is true?

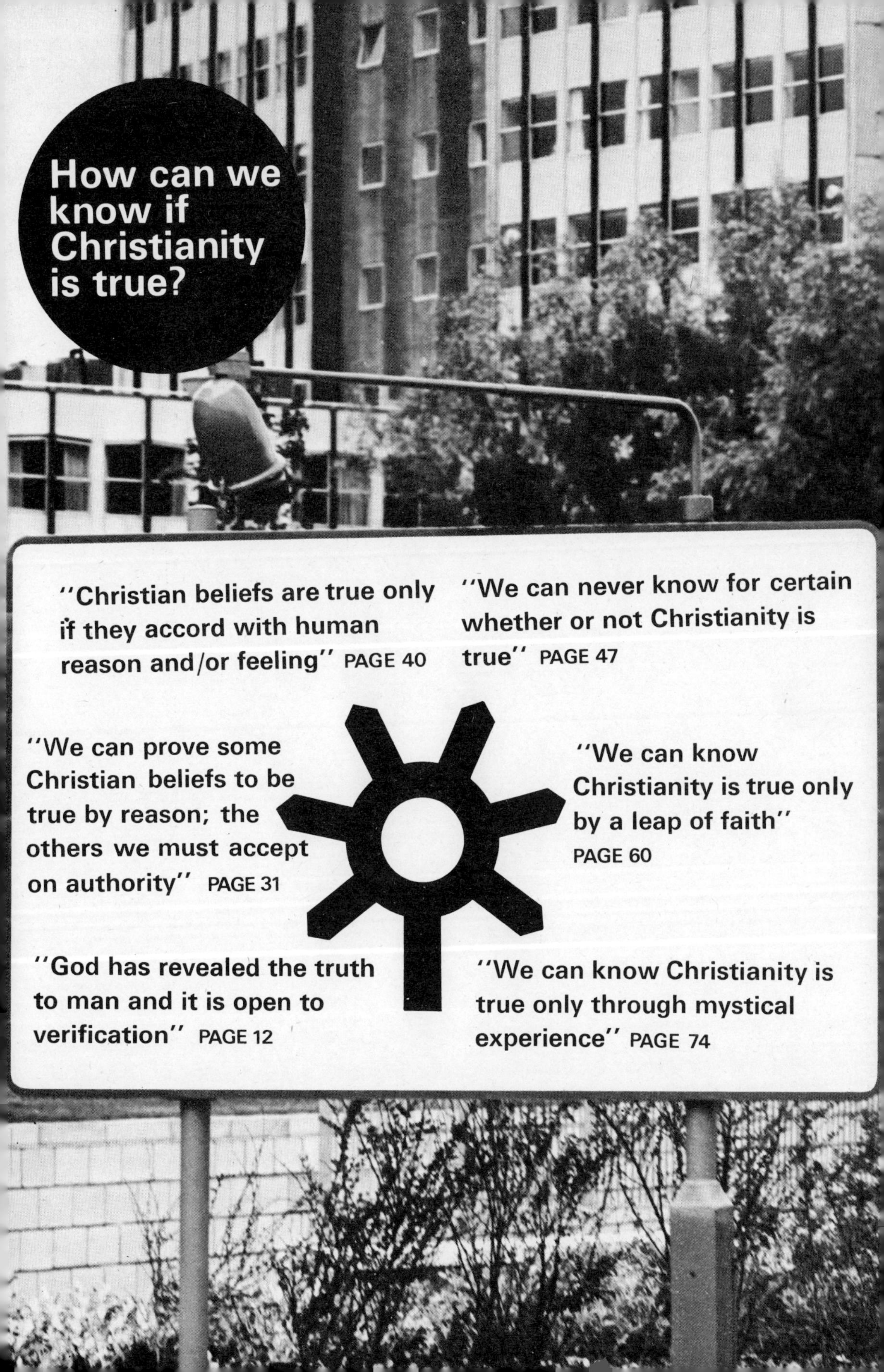

"Christian beliefs are true only if they accord with human reason and/or feeling" PAGE 40

"We can never know for certain whether or not Christianity is true" PAGE 47

"We can prove some Christian beliefs to be true by reason; the others we must accept on authority" PAGE 31

"We can know Christianity is true only by a leap of faith" PAGE 60

"God has revealed the truth to man and it is open to verification" PAGE 12

"We can know Christianity is true only through mystical experience" PAGE 74

1. THE ANSWER OF BIBLICAL CHRISTIANITY

"God has revealed the truth to man and it is open to verification"

The Christianity of the Bible claims that:

☐ **God has revealed the truth about himself, the universe and man;**

☐ **The truth he has revealed is open to verification.**

These two parts of the answer need to be taken very closely together.

GOD HAS REVEALED THE TRUTH

The Bible points to four different ways in which God has revealed truth to men: through the universe; through the nature of man; through the written word of God in the Bible; and above all through Jesus Christ.

Revelation through the universe

The universe tells us something about the God who made it. The character of the universe – its size, its complexity, its order and its beauty – tell us something about the Creator. It is not a revelation in words, but the universe does, as the psalmist says, 'say' something about God.

The heavens are telling the glory of God;
  and the firmament proclaims his handiwork.
Day to day pours forth speech,
  and night to night declares knowledge.
There is no speech, nor are there words;
  their voice is not heard;
yet their voice goes out through all the earth,
  and their words to the end of the world.

This kind of revelation, however, is limited. It tells us only certain things about God. Job, for example, is very conscious of the limitations of this kind of revelation:

He binds up the waters in his thick clouds,
  and the cloud is not rent under them.
He covers the face of the moon,
  and spreads over it his cloud . . .
Lo, these are but the outskirts of his ways;
  and how small a whisper do we hear of him!

But despite the incompleteness of this revelation, it leaves men with no excuse when they reject and suppress that amount of truth which is clearly revealed. Paul writes:

For the wrath of God is revealed from heaven against all ungodliness and wickedness of men who by their wickedness suppress the truth. For what can be known about God is plain to them, because God has shown it to them. Ever since the creation of the world his invisible nature,

Majestic peaks of mountains in Peru: nature tells us something of the work of a Creator God.

namely, his eternal power and deity, has been clearly perceived in the things that have been made. So they are without excuse . . .

Richard Wurmbrand tells the story of how this kind of thinking about the universe occurred to a Russian couple who were both sculptors and had been brought up to believe that there is no God:

Once, we worked on a statue of Stalin. During the work, my wife asked me: "Husband, how about the thumb? If we could not oppose the thumb to the other fingers – if the fingers of the hands were like toes – we could not hold a hammer, a mallet, any tool, a book, a piece of bread. Human life would be impossible without this little thumb. Now, who has made the thumb? We both learned Marxism in school and know that heaven and earth exist by themselves. They are not created by God. So I have learned and so I believe. But if God did not create heaven and

earth, if he created only the thumb, he would be praiseworthy for this little thing.

"We praise Edison and Bell and Stephenson who have invented the electric bulb, the telephone and the railway and other things. But why should we not praise the one who has invented the thumb? If Edison had not had a thumb he would have invented nothing. It is only right to worship God who has made the thumb." '

The husband became very angry ... 'Don't speak stupidities! You have learned that there is no God. And you can never know if the house is not bugged and if we will not fall into trouble. Get into your mind *once and for all* that there is no God. In heaven there is *nobody!*'

She replied: 'This is an even greater wonder. If in heaven there were the Almighty God in whom in stupidity our forefathers believed, it would be only natural that we should have thumbs. An Almighty God can do everything, so he can make a thumb, too. But if in heaven there is nobody, I, from my side, am decided to worship from all my heart the "Nobody" who had made the thumb.'

Revelation through the nature of man

Everyone in certain situations has feelings that are described by the word 'ought':

'You ought to do this' or 'You ought not to do that'.

'I ought to do this' or 'I ought not to do that'.

None of us is so completely amoral that we feel that anything can be allowed and nothing discouraged.

Different societies have different social codes and different laws; but there is a large measure of agreement between them. The moral codes of the great religions have much in common with each other.

According to Christian beliefs, man is a fallen creature, and his conscience therefore does not invariably reflect the will of God. But at many points his own instincts correspond very closely with what God has revealed in a fuller way through the written word in the Bible and through Jesus Christ.

Christianity says that these basic instincts reveal something, however dimly, of the character of the God who has made man in his likeness. They are not simply the product of the society and the culture in which man lives. Furthermore, when we expect others to accept our standards, or judge others by our standards, we are assuming that these standards are right, and consistent with the way things are. This in itself points to the existence of a personal God who has made things this way. Paul's letter to the Romans puts it like this:

Therefore you have no excuse, O man, whoever you are, when you judge another; for in passing judgment upon him you condemn yourself, because you, the judge, are doing the very same things ...
When the Gentiles who have not the law do by nature what the law requires, they are a law to themselves, even though they do not have the law. They show that what the law requires is written on their hearts, while their conscience also bears witness and their conflicting thoughts accuse or perhaps excuse them ...

These two kinds of revelation, however, are limited. The universe does not tell us anything about the moral character of God, or whether he is a loving God or a cruel God. And the sinfulness of man frequently blinds him to the limited amount of truth which he knows from his own nature.

Revelation through the written word of God in the Bible

Belief in the Bible as a revelation of God is based on three things:

▷ **The claims of parts of the Old Testament.** Many of the Old Testament writers speak of God revealing himself *both* through his actions *and* through his words, *i.e.* by what he does in history, and by what he reveals in words communicated to the minds of the prophets.

The Lord used to speak to Moses face to face, as a man speaks to his friend.

Surely the Lord God does nothing,
without revealing his secret to his servants the prophets.

Sometimes we are told that those who received this revelation wrote down what had been revealed:

Moses came and told the people all the words of the Lord and all the ordinances; and all the people answered with one voice, and said, 'All the words which the Lord has spoken we will do.' And Moses wrote all the words of the Lord.

Then the Lord put forth his hand and touched my mouth; and the Lord said to me,

'Behold, I have put my words in your mouth.

See, I have set you this day over nations and over kingdoms . . .'

And the word of the Lord came to me, saying, 'Jeremiah, . . .'

Then Jeremiah called Baruch the son of Neriah, and Baruch wrote upon a scroll at the dictation of Jeremiah all the words of the Lord which he had spoken to him.

This is how the writer of Psalm 119 speaks about the writings of the scriptures which he had at that time:

thy precepts (verse 4)
thy statutes (verse 5)
thy commandments (verse 6)
thy righteous ordinances (verse 7)
thy word (verse 9)
the ordinances of thy mouth (verse 13)
thy testimonies (verse 14)
thy law (verse 18)
thy promise (verse 38)
thy words (verse 57)

The New Testament writers believed that the Old Testament had the highest possible authority:

In many and various ways God spoke of old to our fathers by the prophets . . .

No prophecy ever came by the impulse of man, but men moved by the Holy Spirit spoke from God.

▷ **The claims of Jesus for parts of the Old Testament and for the Old Testament as a whole.** While Jesus himself claimed to be a fuller revelation of God, he did not question the truth or the authority of what had already been revealed through the Old Testament. He assumed it had the highest possible authority and used it to explain his own authority.

Think not that I have come to abolish the law and the prophets; I have come not to abolish them but to fulfil them. For truly, I say to you, till heaven and earth pass away, not an iota, not a dot, will pass from the law until all is accomplished. Whoever then relaxes one of the least of these commandments and teaches men so, shall be called least in the kingdom of heaven; but he who does them and teaches them shall be called great in the kingdom of heaven.

Jesus answered them, 'Is it not written in your law, "I said, you are gods"? If he called them gods to whom the word of God came (and scripture cannot be broken), do you say of him whom the Father consecrated and sent into the world, "You are blaspheming," because I said, "I am the Son of God"?'

You search the scriptures, because you think that in them you have eternal life; and it is they that bear witness to me.

This is how Jesus speaks about the authority of certain specific parts of the Old Testament:

And as Jesus taught in the temple, he said, 'How can the scribes say that the Christ is the son of David? David himself, inspired by the Holy Spirit, declared,

"The Lord said to my Lord,

Sit at my right hand,

till I put thy enemies under thy feet." '

And Pharisees came up to him and tested him by asking, 'Is it lawful to divorce one's wife for any cause?' He answered, 'Have you not read that he who made them from the beginning made them male and female, and said, "For this reason a man shall leave his father and mother and be joined to his wife, and the two shall become one"?'

Then he said to them, 'These are my words which I spoke to you, while I was still with you, that everything written about me in the law of Moses and the prophets and the psalms must be fulfilled.' Then he opened their minds to understand the scriptures.

▷ **The authority which Jesus gave the apostles.** Jesus promised his disciples that the Holy Spirit would enable them to give a reliable account of his teaching, and would show them more of the truth which would be revealed later. This promise was primarily for the apostles themselves.

The Counsellor, the Holy Spirit, whom the Father will send in my name, he will teach you all things, and bring to your remembrance all that I have said to you.

I have yet many things to say to you, but you cannot bear them now. When the Spirit of truth comes, he will guide you into all the truth; for he will not speak on his own authority, but whatever he hears he will speak, and he will declare to you the things that are to come.

One of the earliest existing New Testament manuscripts is this 3rd-4th century papyrus roll, showing part of the Epistle to the Hebrews.

Paul claimed that he too had been commissioned as an apostle—in his case, through the exceptional circumstances of his conversion. He believed that the Holy Spirit had revealed the truth to him in specific words:

Now we have received not the spirit of the world, but the Spirit which is from God, that we might understand the gifts bestowed on us by God. And we impart this in words not taught by human wisdom but taught by the Spirit, interpreting spiritual truths to those who possess the Spirit.

Any claim to a new revelation must be tested by the standard of what he and the other apostles taught; and if it conflicted with it, it must be rejected.

I am astonished that you are so quickly deserting him who called you in the grace of Christ and turning to a different gospel – not that there is another gospel, but there are some who trouble you and want to pervert the gospel of Christ. But even if we, or an angel from heaven, should preach to you a gospel contrary to that which we preached to you, let him be accursed. As we have said before, so now I say again, If any one is preaching to you a gospel contrary to that which you received, let him be accursed.

Follow the pattern of the sound words which you have heard from me, in the faith and love which are in Christ Jesus; guard the truth that has been entrusted to you by the Holy Spirit who dwells within us.

Revelation through Jesus Christ

Jesus spoke of himself as the one who reveals the Father:

All things have been delivered to me by my Father; and no one knows the Son except the Father, and no one knows the Father except the Son and any one to whom the Son chooses to reveal him.

Jesus said to him, 'I am the way, and the truth, and the life; no one comes to the Father, but by me. If you had known me, you would have known my Father also; henceforth you know him and have seen him.'

Philip said to him, 'Lord, show us the Father, and we shall be satisfied.' Jesus said to him, 'Have

I been with you so long, and yet you do not know me, Philip? He who has seen me has seen the Father; how can you say, "Show us the Father"? Do you not believe that I am in the Father and the Father in me? . . .'

This is the comment of one of the disciples who knew Jesus:

Grace and truth came through Jesus Christ. No one has ever seen God; the only Son, who is in the bosom of the Father, he has made him known.

The writer of the letter to the Hebrews links together God's revelation of himself through the prophets in the Old Testament with his revelation of himself in Jesus Christ:

In many and various ways God spoke of old to our fathers by the prophets; but in these last days he has spoken to us by a Son.

To say that God has revealed the truth does not mean that he has revealed *everything* there is to be known. The revelation he has given in these four ways is not exhaustive, but it is adequate. We can be sure that what has *not* been revealed is not inconsistent in any way with what *has* been revealed. What we still have to learn about God will not contradict what we already know about him.

Moses, for example, makes a distinction between what has been revealed and what has not been revealed. What has been revealed provides an adequate basis for living both here and now, and in the future:

The secret things belong to the Lord our God; but the things that are revealed belong to us and to our children for ever, that we may do all the words of this law.

Similarly, Paul contrasts his present knowledge of God with the knowledge he will have in heaven:

Now we see in a mirror dimly, but then face to face. Now I know in part; then I shall understand fully, even as I have been fully understood.

The incompleteness of his knowledge in this life, however, does not make him sceptical or agnostic. He believes that the truth which has already been revealed is utterly reliable and trustworthy:

We have received . . . the Spirit which is from God, that we might understand the gifts bestowed on us by God. And we impart this in words not taught by human wisdom but taught by the Spirit.

If anyone thinks that he is a prophet, or spiritual, he should acknowledge that what I am writing to you is a command of the Lord.

THE TRUTH GOD HAS REVEALED IS OPEN TO VERIFICATION

In the course of the revelation, there were certain vital points where the people involved were able to verify what came to them as a revelation from God. If the word 'verification' sounds a very modern word, this does not mean that the idea is modern. All through the Bible we find that men are concerned with the basic question: how can I *know* if this is true? They were not prepared to believe any and every miracle or revelation which purported to be from God.

▷ **Abraham** is promised by God that he will be the ancestor of a great nation, and that his descendants will inherit the land of Canaan. At first he simply believes the promise; he takes it on trust. But then he asks for some more definite assurance that the promise will be fulfilled:

He (God) brought him outside and said, 'Look toward heaven, and number the stars, if you are able to number them.' Then he said to him, 'So shall your descendants be.' And he *believed* the Lord; and he reckoned it to him as righteousness. And he said to him, 'I am the Lord who brought you from Ur of the Chaldeans to give you this land to possess.' But he said, 'O Lord God, *how am I to know* that I shall possess it?' . . .

The account then goes on to describe something which God did before Abraham's eyes.

Then the Lord said to Abram, '*Know of a surety that your descendants will be sojourners in a land that is not theirs ... And they shall come back here in the fourth generation ...*'

▷ When **Moses** meets God in the wilderness, he is commissioned to lead his people out of slavery in Egypt. Moses' reply has a very contemporary ring about it:

Then Moses answered, 'But behold, they *will not believe me* or listen to my voice, for they will say, "The Lord did not appear to you." ' The Lord said to him, 'What is that in your hand?' He said, 'A rod.' ...

God then performs a miracle with the rod which Moses has in his hand; and the purpose of the miracle is:

that they may *believe* that the Lord, the God of their fathers, the God of Abraham, the God of Isaac, and the God of Jacob, has appeared to you ... If they will not believe you ... or heed the first sign, they may believe the latter sign. If they will not believe even these two signs or heed your voice, you shall take some water from the Nile and pour it upon the dry ground; and the water which you shall take from the Nile will become blood upon the dry ground.

▷ When **Pharaoh** refuses to let the people go, Moses prophesies that there will be various plagues, and then points to these as evidence for his claims about God's revelation to him:

Thus says the Lord, 'By this *you shall know* that I am the Lord ...'

Each of the subsequent plagues is prophesied with this intention:

that you may *know* that there is no one like the Lord our God ...
that you may *know* that I am the Lord in the midst of the earth.

▷ The record of the events at **Mount Sinai** includes several miracles which were witnessed by all the people. This is how Moses reminds the people, at a later stage, of the events at Mount Sinai:

Take heed ... lest you forget the things which your eyes have *seen* ... how on the day that you stood before the Lord your God at Horeb, the Lord said to me, 'Gather the people to me, that

I may let them *hear* my words, so that they may learn to fear me all the days that they live upon the earth, and that they may teach their children so.' And you came near and stood at the foot of the mountain ... wrapped in darkness, cloud and gloom. Then the Lord spoke to you out of the midst of the fire; you *heard* the sound of words, but saw no form; there was only a voice. And he declared to you his covenant, which he commanded you to perform, that is, the ten commandments; and he wrote them upon two tables of stone.

▷ **Elijah and the priests of Baal** witness one of the most striking examples of verification in the Old Testament. It comes at a time of crisis in the history of the Children of Israel, when false ideas of God associated with Baal have become very popular. Elijah, the prophet of God, issues a challenge to the prophets of Baal:

And Elijah came near to all the people, and said, 'How long will you go limping with two different opinions? If the Lord is God, follow him; but if Baal, then follow him ... Let two bulls be given to us; and let them choose one bull for themselves, and cut it in pieces and lay it on the wood, but put no fire to it; and I will prepare the other bull and lay it on the wood, and put no fire to it. And you call on the name of your god and I will call on the name of the Lord; and the God who answers by fire, he is God.' And all the people answered, 'It is well spoken' ...

The prophets of Baal perform their rituals and call on Baal, but nothing happens. Then:

Elijah the prophet came near and said, 'O Lord, God of Abraham, Isaac, and Israel, *let it be known this day that thou art God* in Israel, and that I am thy servant ... Answer me, O Lord, answer me, that *this people may know that thou, O Lord, art God* ...' Then the fire of the Lord fell, and consumed the burnt offering ... And when all the people saw it, they fell on their faces; and they said, 'The Lord, he is God; the Lord, he is God.'

▷ **The prophets** could never simply assume that everyone would automatically accept every word they said as a revelation from God. This is the test which Moses says should be applied to messages claiming to come from God:

If you say in your heart, '*How may we know* the word which the Lord has not spoken?' – when a prophet speaks in the name of the Lord, if the word does not come to pass or come true, that is a word which the Lord has not spoken; the prophet has spoken it presumptuously, you need not be afraid of him.

The prophet Isaiah prophesies about what God is going to do in history. He says that God is telling them what will happen in advance, so that they can be quite certain that he has done it and that he has given the message to the prophet:

... that men may *see* and *know*,
  may consider and understand together,
that the hand of the Lord has done this,
  the Holy One of Israel has created it.

The former things I declared of old,
  they went forth from my mouth and I made
    them known;
  then suddenly I did them and they came to pass.
Because I know that you are obstinate,
  and your neck is an iron sinew,
  and your forehead brass,
I declared them to you from of old,
  before they came to pass I announced them
    to you,
  lest you should say, 'My idol did them ...'

Ezekiel, similarly, predicts what is to happen at different periods of the future; and in each case the intention is that through the prediction and the event following, men may *know*:

... and you shall *know* that I am the Lord.

▷ **The first disciples** came to believe in Jesus gradually, through being with him and working with him over a period of three years. There was no sudden surrender or blind commitment; and they did not believe through the private illumination of any one individual. They were persuaded by the combined evidence of the character, teaching and miracles of Jesus.

They had ample opportunity to get to know almost every side of his *character*, and they could observe whether his life was consistent with what he taught.

They were able to test his *teaching* against what they already knew about God from the Old Testament. They came to see that Jesus' claims about himself were consistent with what God had already revealed.

Lord, to whom shall we go? You have the words of eternal life; and we have *believed*, and have come to *know*, that you are the Holy One of God.

His *miracles* provided further evidence of his unique relationship with God and confirmed the claims he made for himself.

This, the first of his signs, Jesus did at Cana in Galilee, and manifested his glory; and his disciples *believed* in him.

The climax of this evidence was the resurrection. When Thomas refused to accept the word of the other disciples that they had seen the risen Christ, and when he insisted on being able to verify the story before he believed, the risen Christ appeared to him and invited him to touch him, to assure himself that Christ really had been raised from death:

Eight days later, his disciples were again in the house, and Thomas was with them. The doors were shut, but Jesus came and stood among them, and said, 'Peace be with you.' Then he said to Thomas, 'Put your finger here, and see my hands; and put out your hand, and place it in my side; do not be faithless, but believing.' Thomas answered him, 'My Lord and my God!'

▷ **The early preaching about Jesus.** *Peter* first preached about Jesus in Jerusalem, seven weeks after the resurrection. He could assume that his audience had heard the reports of what had happened and, if they wanted to, could check them for themselves by questioning those involved. All he need do therefore was to remind them of what had happened, and interpret its meaning:

Men of Israel, hear these words: Jesus of Nazareth, a man attested to you by God with mighty works and wonders and signs which God did through him in your midst, as you yourselves know – this Jesus, delivered up according to the definite plan and foreknowledge of God, you crucified and killed by the hands of lawless men ... This Jesus God raised up, and of that we all are witnesses ... Let all the house of Israel therefore know assuredly that God has made him both Lord and Christ, this Jesus whom you crucified.

Paul, in one of the earliest parts of the New Testament to be written, reminds the

Corinthians in simple outline of the events of the resurrection:

I delivered to you as of first importance what I also received, that Christ died for our sins in accordance with the scriptures, that he was buried, that he was raised on the third day in accordance with the scriptures, and that he appeared to Cephas, then to the twelve. Then he appeared to more than five hundred brethren at one time, most of whom are still alive, though some have fallen asleep. Then he appeared to James, then to all the apostles. Last of all . . . he appeared also to me.

In this context Paul is saying in effect, 'If you want to check up on the facts, go and ask any of the eyewitnesses for yourselves. There are many still alive who claim to have seen what happened. Go and verify the story for yourself.'

Luke explains his purpose in writing his Gospel in this way:

Inasmuch as many have undertaken to compile a narrative of the things which have been accomplished among us, just as they were delivered to us by those who from the beginning were eyewitnesses and ministers of the word, it seemed good to me also, having followed all things closely for some time past, to write an orderly account for you, most excellent Theophilus, that you may know the truth concerning the things of which you have been informed.

From this carefully worded introduction, we learn several significant things:

▷ Many people before Luke had attempted to make some kind of record or narrative about the life of Jesus. They were not writing exhaustive records, but they were interested in recording what had happened.

▷ Luke does not claim to have been an eyewitness himself, but he does claim to have been in close touch with those who were.

When the first Christians preached the resurrection, their hearers could check for themselves that the tomb was empty: a first-century rock tomb with rolling stone. SEE BOOK THREE.

▷ Luke wants his reader, Theophilus, to know the truth about the reports he has heard. In his companion volume, the Acts of the Apostles, Luke describes for Theophilus the beginnings of the Christian church after the resurrection. The last part of the book describes in detail the arrest of Paul and his various trials; and it ends with Paul in Rome on trial for his life.

If Theophilus was not actually involved in Paul's trial in some way, he must at least have been interested in it for some reason. And it seems that Luke is simply trying to explain the facts about the origin of Christianity and of how Paul came to be arrested and brought to Rome for trial. He is writing for a contemporary, and much of what he says would be open to verification. If Theophilus wanted to, he could check up on the details – the various Roman authorities Luke mentions, and so on.

CAN CHRISTIAN BELIEFS BE VERIFIED TODAY?

We are no longer in a position to carry out precisely the same tests that people involved in the biblical events were able to carry out.

But if we are familiar with what verification means in science, history and philosophy, and even in personal relationships, we can see how the approach to establishing truth in each of these areas can be applied to Christian beliefs.

Scientific verification

This is how *Jacob Bronowski* describes the principle of verification in science:

We cannot shirk the historic question, What is truth? On the contrary: the civilization we take pride in took a new strength on the day the question was asked. It took its greatest strength later from Renaissance men like Leonardo, in whom truth to fact became a passion. The sanction of experienced fact as a face of truth is ... the mainspring which has moved our civilization since the Renaissance.

The first step is the collection of data ... Next comes the creative step ... which finds an order in the data by exploring likenesses ... and the third step is to create this concept (the central concept) ... This sequence is characteristic of science. It begins with a set of appearances. It organizes these into laws. And at the centre of the laws it finds a knot, a point at which several laws cross: a symbol which gives unity to the laws themselves. Mass, time, magnetic moment, the unconscious ... And we test the concept, as we test the thing, by its implications. That is, when the concept has been built up from some experiences, we reason what behaviour in other experiences should logically flow from it. If we find this behaviour, we go on holding the concept as it is. If we do not find the behaviour which the concept logically implies, then we must go back and correct it. In this way logic and experiment are locked together in the scientific method, in a constant to and fro in which each follows the other.

Science is the creation of concepts and their exploration in the facts. It has no other test of the concept than its empirical truth to fact. Truth is the drive at the centre of science; it must have the habit of truth, not as a dogma but as a process.

The test of truth is the known factual evidence ...

We must be careful, however, not to make exaggerated claims about verification in science. Scientists in recent years have become much more modest in their claims for the experimental method. Karl Popper, for example, has suggested that we should think of the experimental method as a method of *disproof* rather than proof.

John Wren-Lewis summarizes Karl Popper's views in this way:

It does *not* mean 'proving your theories by experimental test'. It is a commonplace in philosophy that nothing can ever be proved by experimental test, because an infinite number of tests would be required. What you *can* do is to *disprove* theories, and the essential feature of the experimental method is that it sets up artificial situations especially designed to disprove the chosen theory if possible ...

The experimental method involves treating theories as *formulae for communicating possible innovations* rather than as intuitions of deeper truth.

Dr Jacob Bronowski

Historic Christianity has always believed that the universe was created by God and is sustained by God; and that man is different from the animals in that he bears 'the image of God'. These beliefs must inevitably have some point of contact with the theories of various sciences, and especially about the origin of the universe and man.

If we accept biblical Christianity's answer to the question 'how can we know if Christianity is true?' we also accept the challenge of the scientist. We have to reply, 'What you say about the scientific method *is* relevant in considering the truth of Christianity. What we must do is to approach Christian beliefs about the origin and nature of man and the universe *as one possible theory among many*. And then we simply try to find out which of these theories accounts best for *all* that we know about man and the universe.'

It can hardly be emphasized strongly enough that the question here is not simply: Did man evolve from the apes? This question is important, but it is not the only question; and it must be considered in the context of the much larger question: which of these two ways of thinking about the universe fits the facts better:

that the universe is a completely closed system of cause and effect; that there is no supernatural God; that all there is is what can be seen; and that the universe is the product of chance which has somehow produced purpose;

or that the universe was created by God and depends for its existence on God; that man is what he is because he is stamped with God's likeness?

These two ways of thinking are completely incompatible, and we are forced to make a decisive choice between them. And this choice is far more fundamental than the choice we make about the specific question of the evolution of man.

The process of choosing between these two hypotheses can follow the scientific method closely, step by step. Just as the scientific method depends on presuppositions, observation, theory and experiment, so in the same way in verifying Christian beliefs, presuppositions, observation, theory and experiment all play their part.

Presuppositions

Just as the scientist has presuppositions which he accepts but cannot prove with complete certainty . . .

So in the same way we are bound to approach Christian beliefs with our own presuppositions; *e.g.* that miracles can or cannot happen.

Observation

Just as the scientist must consider all the possible evidence (or as much of it as possible) . . .

So in the same way we must consider all the relevant evidence for Christian beliefs (or as much of it as possible)—and this will include the evidence about the origin of the universe and of man, and also the total experience of others and ourselves.

Theory

Just as the scientist considers all the possible theories and tries to find the theory or hypothesis which accounts best for all that he observes; *e.g.* which theory makes the best sense of the data that we observe:
—that the sun goes round the earth?
—or that the earth goes round the sun? . . .

So in the same way we must try to find the theory which fits the facts best; *i.e.* which theory makes the best sense of what we observe in the universe and in man:
—that the universe is a completely closed system of cause and effect, the product of impersonal energy, time and chance?
—or that the universe was created by an infinite, personal God?

Experiment

Just as the scientist must conduct the necessary experiments to test all the possible theories, and to eliminate false theories . . .

So in the same way we can test these rival beliefs by the test of fact; *i.e.* by observing what happens when one lives consistently on the basis of one or other of these beliefs.

As an example of a non-Christian who accepts this method of discussing beliefs about man and the universe, we may quote *Bronowski, Science and Human Values*. The Christian will not agree with the *conclusion* at which he arrives; but his *method* is precisely the same as that which has been outlined here:

. . . Does this (concept) really work . . . without force, without corruption, and without another arbitrary superstructure of laws which do not derive from the central concept? Do its consequences fit our experience; do men in such a society live so or not so? This is the simple but profound test of fact by which we have come to judge the large words of the makers of states and systems.

There have always been two ways of looking for truth. One is to find concepts which are beyond challenge, because they are held by faith or by authority or the conviction that they are self-evident. This is the mystic submission to truth which the East has chosen, and which dominated the axiomatic thought of the scholars of the Middle Ages. So St Thomas Aquinas holds that faith is a higher guide to truth than knowledge is; the master of medieval science puts science firmly into second place.

But long before Aquinas wrote, Peter Abelard had already challenged the whole notion that there are concepts which can only be felt by faith or authority. All truth, even the highest, is accessible to test, said Abelard: 'By doubting we are led to inquire, and by inquiry we perceive the truth'. . . .

The habit of testing and correcting the concept by its consequences in experience has been the spring within the movement of our civilization ever since. In science and in art and in self-knowledge we explore and move constantly by turning to the world of sense to ask, Is this so? This is the habit of truth . . .

Science is indeed a truthful activity. And whether we look at facts, at things, or at concepts, we cannot disentangle truth from meaning—that is, from an inner order. Truth therefore is not different in science and in the arts; the facts of the heart, the bases of personality, are merely more difficult to communicate. Truth to fact is the same habit in both, and has the same importance for both, because facts are the only raw material from which we can derive a change of mind. In science, the appeal to fact is the exploration of the concept in its logical consequences. In the arts, the emotional facts fix the limits of experience which can be shared in their language.

This approach is worked out in greater detail in question three, 'Man', and four, 'The Universe', in Book Two.

Historical verification

When we think of verification in historical enquiry, we soon realize that there are many different levels or degrees of certainty. For instance, we cannot reach the same kind of certainty in history as in mathematics. We can illustrate some of these different levels of certainty in this way:

CERTAIN—that Winston Churchill is dead.
—that there was a Second World War.

PROBABLE—that Hitler committed suicide in 1945.
—that in 1700 the population of Scotland was just over one million.

POSSIBLE—that James IV was not killed at the battle of Flodden.
—that Queen Elizabeth was really a man (a recent theory).
—that Richard III did not murder the Princes in the Tower.
—that Conan Doyle was Jack the Ripper (a recent suggestion).

IMPROBABLE—that Jesus visited the south of England (an old tradition).
—that Bacon wrote Shakespeare's plays.

The modern historian is not as confident as his predecessors about his ability to reconstruct 'what really happened'. And even assuming that he has got the facts right, he is much more conscious of the difficulty of interpreting them objectively.

Aldous Huxley:

Alas! There is no such thing as Historical Truth —there are only more or less probable opinions about the past, opinions which change from generation to generation. History is a function, mathematically speaking, of the degree of ignorance and of the personal prejudices of historians. The history of any epoch which has left very few documents is at the mercy of archaeological research; a happy discovery may necessitate its radical revision from one day to the next.

Pieter Geyl:

To expect from history those final conclusions, which may perhaps be obtained in other disciplines, is, in my opinion, to misunderstand its nature . . . The scientific method serves above all to establish facts; there is a great deal about which we can reach agreement by its use. But as soon as there is a question of explanation, of interpretation, of appreciation, though the special method of the historian remains valuable, the personal element can no longer be ruled out —that point of view which is determined by the circumstances of his time and by his own preconceptions. No human intelligence can hope to bring together the overwhelming multiplicity of dates and of factors, of forces and movements, and from them establish the true, one might almost say the divine balance. This is literally a superhuman task. A man's judgement—for however solemnly some people may talk about the lessons of History, the historian is after all only a man sitting at his desk—a historian's judgement, then, may seem to him the only possible conclusion to draw from the facts, he may feel himself sustained and comforted by his sense of kinship with the past, and yet that judgement will have no finality. Its truth will be relative, it will be partial. Truth, though for God it may be One, assumes many shapes to men. Thus it is that the analysis of so many conflicting opinions concerning one historical phenomenon is not just a means of whiling away the time, nor need it lead to discouraging conclusions concerning the untrustworthiness of historical study. The study, even of contradictory conceptions can be fruitful . . . History is indeed an argument without end.

Aldous Huxley, English novelist and philosopher.

Some of the beliefs of Christianity are beliefs that certain events happened at particular places and at particular times. These beliefs therefore must be open to the ordinary methods of historical enquiry. Thus:

Just as the historian asks questions about events; *e.g.* did the Battle of Hastings take place or did it not? And if it did happen, did it happen in the way in which the different accounts suggest?

So in the same way we can and must ask questions about the events recorded in the Bible; *e.g.* Did Jesus rise from the dead or did he not? And if he did, did it happen in the way that the documents suggest?

Just as the historian is concerned about the interpretation of events, and asks such questions as: what were the causes of the Second World War? . . .

So in the same way we can ask such questions as: how are we to account for the origin and growth of Christianity?

Just as in attempting to answer these questions, the historian can never be 100% objective, but is inevitably influenced by his presuppositions; *e.g.* Marxist theory . . .

So in the same way in considering the biblical documents we are bound to be influenced by our presuppositions; *e.g.* that miracles can, or cannot, happen.

Just as the historian realizes that he cannot arrive at 100% certainty about the past but is content to accept lesser degrees of certainty . . .

So in the same way while we may not be 100% certain about the events in the Bible, we need not therefore be completely sceptical, discounting the possibility of knowing anything about what happened.

Just as historical events and theories are open to falsification; *i.e.* they can be shown to be highly unlikely or improbable . . .

So in the same way the events recorded in the Bible are open to falsification; they are not immune from historical enquiry.

The Christian does not claim to be able to prove with 100% certainty that Jesus rose from the dead. What he can say is that there are very good historical reasons for believing that he did. He can point out that the documentary evidence for the resurrection is at least as good as the evidence for other events of the period which are never questioned, and very much better than some.

We must therefore examine the evidence for the resurrection and decide where we would place it on the scale of the different degrees of certainty: certain, probable, possible, improbable . . . This approach is worked out in question seven (Book Three) – 'Did Jesus rise from the dead?'

The following quotations from three Christian writers show the place which historical verification has played or still plays in their faith.

C. S. Lewis, speaking about one stage in his conversion:

Early in 1926 the hardest boiled of all the atheists I ever knew sat in my room on the other side of the fire and remarked that the evidence for the historicity of the Gospels was really surprisingly good. 'Rum thing,' he went on. 'All that stuff of Frazer's about the Dying God. Rum thing. It almost looks as if it had really happened once!'

Frank Morison set out to prove that the resurrection did not happen, but through his study of the evidence was forced to change his mind:

A study by Tom Blau of C. S. Lewis, author and Professor of Medieval and Renaissance English at Cambridge.

I wanted to take this Last Phase of the life of Jesus, with all its quick and pulsating drama, its sharp, clear-cut, background of antiquity, and its tremendous psychological and human interest —to strip it of its overgrowth of primitive beliefs and dogmatic suppositions, and to see this supremely great Person as He really was.
... Fully ten years later, the opportunity came to study the life of Christ as I had long wanted to study it, to investigate the origins of its literature, to sift some of the evidence at first hand, and to form my own judgement on the problem which it presents. I will only say that it effected a revolution in my thought. Things emerged from that old-world story which previously I should have thought impossible. Slowly but very definitely the conviction grew that the drama of those unforgettable weeks of human history was stranger and deeper than it seemed. It was the *strangeness* of many notable things in the story which first arrested and held my interest. It was only later that the irresistible logic of their meaning came into view.

A. R. Vidler refers to *N. P. Williams'* extreme statement of the vulnerability of his faith:

If an ostrakon were unearthed at Nazareth which showed conclusively that Joseph was the father of Jesus, he would abandon the Christian faith and look round for some other theory of the universe.

This approach is worked out in Book Three in the questions about Jesus Christ.

Philosophical verification

Philosophy in the past has generally been concerned with the search for truth. This is how *C. E. M. Joad* sums up the aims of traditional philosophy:

The object of philosophy, as I conceive it, is not to help people, but to discover truth. I want to know *qua* philosopher what the universe is like.

It is the business of philosophy, as I conceive it, to seek to understand the nature of the universe as a whole, not, as do the sciences, some special department of it, but the whole bag of tricks to which the moral feelings of the Puritan, the herd instinct of the man in the street, the religious consciousness of the saint, the aesthetic enjoyment of the artist, the history of the human race and its contemporary follies, no less than the latest discoveries of science contribute. Reflecting upon this mass of data, the philosopher seeks to interpret it. He looks for a clue to guide him through the labyrinth, for a system wherewith to classify, or a purpose in terms of which to make meaningful.

Bertrand Russell:

Is there any knowledge in the world which is so certain that no reasonable man could doubt it? This question, which at first sight might not seem difficult, is really one of the most difficult that can be asked. When we have realized the obstacles in the way of a straightforward and confident answer, we shall be well launched on the study of philosophy—for philosophy is merely the attempt to answer such ultimate questions, not carelessly and dogmatically, as we do in ordinary life and even in the sciences, but critically, after exploring all that makes such questions puzzling, and after realizing all the vagueness and confusion that underlie our ordinary ideas.

In philosophy, a belief is considered to be 'true' if it corresponds to the facts. There are two stages in the process of verification:

First, does it make sense? Does it contradict itself in any way? Does it violate the basic rule of logic, the law of non-contradiction (that *a* cannot be *non-a*)?

Alasdair MacIntyre:

It is of the essence of assertions that they declare one state of affairs to hold at the expense of others: to assert that an object is one colour is to exclude it from being all other colours; to assert that someone is kind and good is to exclude their being cruel or countenancing cruelty. Thus it is a condition of a given utterance being an assertion that there are certain states of affairs which it excludes: and if we find that such a state of affairs does in fact hold, the assertion will be false. So in order for an utterance to be an assertion and to be understood as one, it must be capable of falsity. A meaningful assertion must be falsifiable.

Nicolaus Copernicus (1473–1543), Polish astronomer and priest, changed the entire scientific outlook of his day by discovering that the planets revolve round the sun. Basil Willey describes the profound effect his discoveries had on seventeenth-century philosophy: 'Since the advent of the Copernican theory . . . it had been brought home with increasing emphasis that things are not what they seem . . . sense-data, as well as authoritative teaching, were found to be misleading . . .'

(The original form of the Verification Principle put forward by the Vienna Circle of Linguistic Philosophers, stated that a proposition is meaningful *only* if it is open to verification; if it is not open to any kind of verification, then it does not make sense, and we cannot even begin to ask whether it is true or not. This principle can hardly be applied consistently, because the principle itself is not open to verification; and therefore on its own terms cannot make sense, let alone be true.)

Second, does it fit the facts? Does it correspond to our experience, our knowledge?

Bertrand Russell:

Philosophical knowledge ... does not differ essentially from scientific knowledge; there is no special source of wisdom which is open to philosophy but not to science ... Philosophy, like all other studies, aims primarily at knowledge.

It is customary to say that a general proposition is 'verified' when all of its consequences which it has been possible to test have been found to be true.

Truth is a property of beliefs, and derivatively of sentences which express beliefs. Truth consists in a certain relation between a belief and one or more facts other than the belief. When this relation is absent, the belief is false. A sentence may be called 'true' or 'false' even if no one believes it, provided that if it were to be believed, the belief would be true or false as the case may be.

To say, therefore, that Christian beliefs are open to verification means that Christian beliefs can be discussed on the same level as philosophical beliefs. Therefore:

Just as philosophers ask 'Does this theory make sense? Is it consistent with itself? Does it contradict itself?' ...

So in the same way we can and must ask 'Does this Christian belief make sense? Is it consistent with itself? Does it contradict itself?'

Just as the philosopher asks 'Is this theory consistent with everything else that I know?' ...

So in the same way we ask 'Is this Christian belief consistent with everything else that I know?'

Just as the philosopher has to use as his data all his own experience and knowledge, and the experience and knowledge of others ...

So in the same way in putting Christian beliefs on trial we can use as evidence all our own experience and knowledge, and the experience and knowledge of others.

Just as a philosophical belief is open to verification and is also open to falsification ...

So in the same way Christian beliefs are open to falsification.

This does not mean that Christian beliefs can be reduced *permanently* to the level of an abstract hypothetical system. But it does mean that we can at least *begin* in this way. We have to ask ourselves whether this system fits the facts better than other beliefs claim to. If we consider them at all seriously, we will soon realize that we cannot remain in the position of the armchair philosopher or the disinterested spectator for ever. For if Christian beliefs *are* true, we have to come to terms with our Creator, and this will have a profound effect on the way we think and feel and behave.

It was through following this approach that *C. E. M. Joad* eventually abandoned his agnosticism and became a Christian. In his book *The Recovery of Belief* he writes:

The following book is an account of some of the reasons which have converted me to the religious view of the universe in its Christian version. They are predominantly arguments designed to appeal to the intellect ...

While I admit that intellect cannot go all the way, there can, for me, be no believing which the intellect cannot, so far as its writ runs, defend and justify. I must, as a matter of psychological compulsion, adopt the most rational hypothesis, the most rational being that which seems to cover most of the facts and to offer the most plausible explanation of our experience as a whole ...

It is because ... the religious view of the universe seems to me to cover more of the facts of experience than any other that I have been gradually led to embrace it ...

What I have to record is a changed view of the nature of man, which in due course led to a changed view of the nature of the world ...

This view of human evil (that evil is merely the product of heredity and environment and can be eradicated through progress) which I adopted unthinkingly as a young man I have come fundamentally to disbelieve. Plausible, perhaps, during the first fourteen years of this century when . . . the state of mankind seemed to be improving—though the most cursory reading of human history should even then have been sufficient to dispose of it—it has been rendered utterly unplausible by the events of the last forty years. To me, at any rate, the view of evil implied by Marxism, expressed by Shaw and maintained by psychotherapy, a view which regards evil as a by-product of circumstances, which circumstances can, therefore, alter and even eliminate, has come to seem intolerably shallow and the contrary view of it as endemic in man, more particularly in its Christian form, the doctrine of original sin, to express a deep and essential insight into human nature.

This approach is worked out in questions two, 'God', three, 'Man' and four, 'The Universe' (Book Two).

Verification in personal relationships

We are not in the habit of associating verification with personal relationships. And many are inclined to drive a wedge between *scientific* knowledge and *personal* knowledge. But we can say that there is a kind of testing going on all the time in our relationships with others; and without this testing, there would soon be a breakdown of understanding or of trust between people. Unless we are incredibly gullible, we do not believe everything that people say, and we do not accept people at their face value without ever raising any questions in our minds. Consciously (or perhaps unconsciously) we notice how people speak and behave, and in this way our estimate of them is either confirmed or revised. One dishonest or cruel action could be quite enough to make us change our minds about someone so that we cease to trust him in the same way.

This means that our faith in people cannot be separated from our knowledge of them. Our belief in them is very closely tied up with what we believe about them. Trust and even love are open to a very real kind of testing.

The process of finding out about Jesus Christ and coming to trust and love him can be basically the same as the process by which we come to trust and love another person. Thus:

Just as we can ask: can I trust *x*? Is he genuine? Is he the kind of person he claims to be? Can he do what he claims to be able to do? . . .

So in the same way we can ask: can I trust Jesus Christ? Is he genuine? Is he the person he claims to be? Can he really do what he claims to be able to do for me?

Just as we receive impressions about a person through observing his behaviour and hearing his words, and through hearing what others say about him . . .

So in the same way we can receive impressions about Jesus through reading about his life and his words, and by hearing the testimony of those who trust him today.

Just as we are hesitant about trusting a person in big things unless we have good reasons for trusting him and have some basis for our confidence in him . . .

So in the same way we are not likely to trust Jesus and enter into a relationship with him unless we have good reasons for trusting him and have some good basis for our confidence.

Just as we cannot expect 100% certainty *before* we trust or love someone, but our trust and love are none the less constantly open to various kinds of tests (since a person's behaviour towards us gives us some indication of his trust or love) . . .

So in the same way we cannot expect 100% certainty *before* we experience the love of Christ for ourselves and come to trust him; but we are not taking a leap in the dark, because at each stage we can test whether his words are genuine and whether he means what he says.

The Bible contains many invitations to put the character and promises of God to the test:

O taste and see that the Lord is good!
   Happy is the man who takes refuge in him!

Offer to God a sacrifice of thanksgiving,
   and pay your vows to the Most High;
and call upon me in the day of trouble;
   I will deliver you, and you shall glorify me.

Bring the full tithes into the storehouse, that there may be food in my house; and thereby put me to the test, says the Lord of hosts, if I will not open the windows of heaven for you and pour down for you an overflowing blessing.

The invitation of Jesus:

Come to me, all who labour and are heavy laden, and I will give you rest. Take my yoke upon you, and learn from me; for I am gentle and lowly in heart, and you will find rest for your souls. For my yoke is easy, and my burden is light.

The Bible also contains the testimony of many who tested the promises of God and verified the truth of his revelation for themselves:

I sought the Lord, and he answered me,
   and delivered me from all my fears.

I love the Lord, because he has heard
   my voice and my supplications.
Because he inclined his ear to me,
   therefore I will call on him as long as I live.

After this many of his disciples drew back and no longer went about with him. Jesus said to the twelve, 'Will you also go away?' Simon Peter answered him, 'Lord, to whom shall we go? You have the words of eternal life; and we have believed, and have come to know, that you are the Holy One of God.'

And the Word became flesh and dwelt among us, full of grace and truth; we have beheld his glory, glory as of the only Son from the Father . . . And from his fullness have we all received, grace upon grace.

Then he said to Thomas, 'Put your finger here, and see my hands; and put out your hand, and place it in my side; do not be faithless, but believing.' Thomas answered him, 'My Lord and my God!'

That which was from the beginning, which we have heard, which we have seen with our eyes, which we have looked upon and touched with our hands, concerning the word of life—the life was made manifest, and we saw it, and testify to it, and proclaim to you the eternal life which was with the Father and was made manifest to us—that which we have seen and heard we proclaim also to you, so that you may have fellowship with us; and our fellowship is with the Father and with his Son Jesus Christ. And we are writing this that our joy may be complete.

Problems and Questions arising out of Biblical Christianity's answer to the question 'How can we know if Christianity is true?' are taken up on p. 79. First we must look at some of the other answers that are given to the basic question.

2. THE ANSWER OF AUTHORITARIANISM

"We can prove some Christian beliefs to be true by reason; the others we must accept on authority"

Scholasticism and traditional Roman Catholic orthodoxy give a two-part answer:

☐ Man can find out some Christian beliefs by his own reason;

☐ The other Christian beliefs are beyond reason; they have been revealed by God, and must be accepted by faith.

Thomas Aquinas (1225–1274):

It was necessary for man's salvation that there should be a doctrine revealed by God, besides the philosophical disciplines investigated by human reason . . . Hence it was necessary for the salvation of man that certain truths which exceed human reason should be made known to him by divine revelation . . .

Therefore, in order that the salvation of men might be brought about more fitly and more surely, it was necessary that they should be taught divine truths by divine revelation. It was therefore necessary that, besides the philosophical disciplines investigated by reason, there should be a sacred doctrine by way of revelation.

Although those things which are beyond man's knowledge may not be sought for by man through his reason, nevertheless, what is revealed by God must be accepted through faith.

MAN CAN FIND OUT SOME CHRISTIAN BELIEFS BY HIS OWN REASON

Man is finite, and he is a fallen creature; but he is still able to arrive at *some* of the truth about God and the universe simply by using his own reason. In this way, for example, he can know:

the existence of God: reason can prove *that* God exists, though it cannot tell us everything we need to know about God.

the existence of the moral law, or natural law, in the conscience.

This answer has led to the way in which the traditional arguments for the existence of God have been formulated. The three basic arguments in their simplest form can be formulated in this way:

The ontological argument

I have an idea of God as the Perfect Being, or as 'that than which nothing greater can be conceived'.

If the idea exists, then the thing itself must exist; the idea must correspond to something which is there outside my mind.

Therefore God must exist.

The cosmological argument

Every effect has a cause.

Therefore there must be a First Cause to create the universe, and God is by definition the First Cause.

Therefore God must exist.

The teleological argument

Anything which shows traces of design must have been designed by some intelligent being.

The universe shows signs of order and design; therefore there must be a Designer; and God is, by definition, the Creator and Designer.

Therefore God exists.

These arguments for the existence of God are still an official part of Roman Catholic teaching:

If anyone says that the one true God, our Creator and Lord, cannot be known with certainty by the natural light of human reason through those things which are made: let him be anathema.

TRUTHS WHICH ARE BEYOND REASON HAVE BEEN REVEALED BY GOD AND MUST BE RECEIVED BY FAITH

The knowledge which we can gain by the use of reason is not complete. We cannot, for example, deduce the Trinity, or belief in salvation through Christ simply by reason.

If these beliefs are beyond reason, we cannot test them in any way by reason. We can ask questions to test the authority which teaches us these truths; but once we have accepted that authority we accept the truth of what it teaches.

For example, Roman Catholicism gives certain reasons for the infallible authority of the church as the teaching institution: *e.g.* the words of Jesus to Peter; the development of the Papacy at Rome. Once we have accepted this authority, we accept what it tells us.

Cardinal Heenan:

This secret of this wonderful unity of our Church is Christ's promise that the Church will never fail to teach the truth. Once we know what the Church teaches we accept it. For we know it must be true . . . All Catholic priests teach the same doctrine because they all obey the Vicar of Christ. The word 'vicar' means 'one who takes the place of another'. The Pope is the Vicar of Christ because he takes the place of Christ as Head of the Church on earth.

The Church remains one because all her members believe the same Faith. They believe it because the Church cannot teach what is false. This is what we mean when we say that the Church is infallible. Christ promised to guide his Church. One of the ways Christ chose to guide the Church was by leaving his Vicar on earth to speak for

Cardinal John Heenan, Archbishop of Westminster and leader of the Roman Catholic Church in Britain since 1963.

The Qur'an: Surah XI, verses 88-107, Arabic decorated manuscript, thirteenth century.

him. That is why we say the Pope is infallible. He is the Head of the infallible Church. God could not allow him to lead it into error

ISLAM

This answer is also the one which Muslims give to the question 'How can I know if Islam is true?' The Muslim believes that God has revealed something of himself in the universe and in the nature of man. But if one asks, 'How can I know if the Qur'an is the word of God, a true revelation from God?' these are the kind of answers which *the Qur'an* itself gives:

▷ Mohammed performed no miracles to prove the truth of his claim to be a prophet. When challenged to produce his credentials, he simply pointed to the unique character of the Qur'an itself. The very fact of the Qur'an itself is therefore sufficient evidence that it is a true revelation from God.

They ask: 'Why has no sign been given him by his Lord?' Say: 'Signs are in the hands of Allah. My mission is only to give plain warning.'
Is it not enough for them that We have revealed to you the Book for their instruction? Surely in this there is a blessing and an admonition to true believers.

This book is not to be doubted. It is a guide to the righteous, who have faith in the unseen and are steadfast in prayer; who bestow in charity a part of what We give them; who trust what has been revealed to you and to others before you, and firmly believe in the life to come . . .

If you doubt what We have revealed to Our Servant, produce one chapter comparable to this book. Call upon your idols to assist you, if what you say be true. But if you fail (as you are sure to fail) then guard yourselves against that fire whose fuel is men and stones prepared for the unbelievers.

▷ Belief and unbelief depend so entirely upon the will of Allah that if he wills a person to believe, he will believe, without any signs. The Qur'an does not seem to admit the possibility that the unbeliever, or even the believer, may have honest doubts and want to ask, 'How can I be sure if it is true?'

The unbelievers ask: 'Why has no sign been given him by his Lord?'
Say: 'Allah leaves in error whom He will, and guides those who repent and have faith; whose

hearts find comfort in the remembrance of Allah. Surely in the remembrance of Allah all hearts are comforted.'

▷ The punishment for unbelief is hell. The threat of hell should bring us to our senses and persuade us to believe.

Those who dispute our revelations shall know that they have no escape.

He has revealed to you the Book with the truth, confirming the scriptures which preceded it; for He has already revealed the Torah and the Gospel for the guidance of men, and the distinction between right and wrong.

Those that deny Allah's revelations shall be sternly punished; Allah is mighty and capable of revenge.

When Our clear revelations are recited to them, the unbelievers say: 'This is plain magic.' Such is their description of the truth when it is declared to them.

Do they say: 'He has invented it himself'? Say: 'If I have indeed invented it, then there is nothing that you can do to save me from Allah's wrath. He well knows what you say about it. He is our all-sufficient witness. He is the Benignant One, the Merciful.'

Say: 'I am no prodigy among the apostles; nor do I know what will be done with me or you. I follow only what is revealed to me, and my only duty is to give plain warning.'

Say: 'Think if this Koran is indeed from Allah and you reject it; if an Israelite has vouched for its divinity and accepted Islam, while you yourselves deny it with scorn. Truly Allah does not guide the wrongdoers.'

The appropriate response, therefore, is simply to listen and obey.

When you do not recite to them a revelation they say: 'Have you not yet invented one?' Say: 'I follow only what is revealed to me by my Lord. This Book is a veritable proof from your Lord, a guide and a blessing to true believers.'

When the Koran is recited, listen to it in silence so that Allah may show you mercy.

It is He who has revealed to you the Koran. Some of its verses are precise in meaning—they are the foundation of the Book—and others ambiguous. Those whose hearts are infected with disbelief follow the ambiguous part, so as to create dissension by seeking to explain it. But no one knows its meaning except Allah. Those who are well-grounded in knowledge say: 'We believe in it: it is from our Lord. But none takes heed except the wise. Lord, do not cause our hearts to go astray after You have guided us.'

PROBLEMS AND QUESTIONS

The traditional arguments for the existence of God are no longer convincing

While Thomas Aquinas' proofs may carry some conviction to those who *already* believe, they mean very little to *the real unbeliever*.

▷ **The conclusion is implied in the premise.** If you accept the first assumption (*e.g.* every effect must have a cause), then the conclusion must follow of necessity. But this is a circular argument. It is similar to this kind of syllogism:

All men are mortal.
Socrates was a man.
Therefore Socrates must be mortal.

▷ **The arguments do not prove enough.** The cosmological argument, for example, would only prove the existence of a First Cause. But it is far too big a jump to move from the First Cause to the God of the Bible. Similarly, the teleological argument points to the existence of a Creator God; but it cannot possibly prove that this Creator must be one God or that he is loving or infinite. The argument does not exclude the possibility that there could be many creator gods, or that God is finite or evil.

▷ **Many people today no longer accept even the premise.** Many people today have the vaguest possible idea of 'God', or have never seriously believed that he exists. For them therefore the idea of a Perfect Being is not obvious or self-evident. Similarly the principle of causality (that every effect has a cause) has been seriously questioned by many philosophers since Hume, and for them this premise is not self-evident. And while some say that they see little or no evidence of order or design in the universe, many others are convinced that evolution by natural selection gives a satisfactory account of the apparent order in nature. Others again do not think of the universe as being ordered; to them it is a product of chance and is basically chaotic and absurd. To them therefore the argument from design does not make sense.

Bronowski sums up the widespread rejection of this approach:

These debates are scholastic exercises in absolute logic. They begin from concepts which are held to be fixed absolutely; they then proceed by deduction; and what is found in this way is subject to no further test. The deductions are true because the first concepts were true: that is the scholastic system.

The two-part answer involves a division of truth

It holds that there are two completely different kinds of truth: truths of reason and truths of revelation. Francis Schaeffer pictures this as a dividing line, with supernatural, religious truth—revealed by God and received by faith—above it, and natural, scientific truth—discovered by man and tested by reason—below:

GRACE
—————
NATURE

This dichotomy of truth became widely accepted by both Protestants and Catholics.

Francis Bacon:

It is therefore most wise soberly to render unto faith the things that are faith's.

Sacred theology must be drawn from the word and oracles of God, not from the light of nature, or the dictates of reason.

(To study theology) we must quit the small vessel of human reason, and put ourselves on board the ship of the Church, which alone possesses the divine needle for justly shaping the course.

We are obliged to believe the word of God, though our reason be shocked at it. For if we should believe only such things as are agreeable to our reason, we assent to the matter, and not to the author.

And therefore, the more absurd and incredible any divine mystery is, the greater honour we do to God in believing it; and so much the more noble the victory of faith.

Thomas Browne:

It is no vulgar part of Faith to believe a thing not only above but contrary to Reason, and against the arguments of our proper senses.

I can answer all the Objections of Satan and my rebellious reason with that odd resolution I learned of Tertullian, *certum est quia impossibile est*.

John Locke:

Reason is the discovery of the certainty or probability of such propositions or truths, which the mind arrives at by deduction made from such *ideas*, which it has got by the use of its natural faculties, *viz.* by sensation or reflection. *Faith* on the other side, is the assent to any proposition not thus made out by the deductions of reason, but upon the credit of the proposer, as coming from God, in some extraordinary way of communication. This way of discovering truths to men we call *Revelation*.

Many who adopted this approach did so with the best of motives; as *Basil Willey* says of Francis Bacon:

What can be asserted with confidence, I think, is that Bacon's desire to separate religious truth and scientific truth was in the interests of science, not of religion. He wished to *keep science pure from religion;* the opposite parts of the process—keeping religion pure from science—did not interest him nearly so much . . . Bacon was pleading for science in an age dominated by religion. Religious truth, then, must be 'skied', elevated far out of reach, not in order that so it may be more devoutly approached, but in order to keep it out of mischief.

In the long run, however, the results were disastrous. The guide and arbiter of truth from now on would be 'natural instinct' and 'common notions' which all men would accept.

Lord Herbert of Cherbury:

Universal consent will be the sovereign test of truth, and there is nothing of so great importance as to seek out these common notions, and to put them each in their place as indubitable truths.

These were some of Herbert's 'common notions':

1. That there is a supreme power.

2. That this sovereign power must be worshipped.

3. That the good ordering or disposition of the faculties of man constitutes the principal or best part of divine worship, and that this has always been believed.

4. That all vices and crimes should be expiated and effaced by repentance.

5. That there are rewards and punishments after this life.

It was not long, therefore, before others began to make greater claims for man's reason, and dispensed with revelation altogether. This kind of answer thus eventually led to the answer of the Rationalists. (See Book Two, on 'Man'.)

Authoritarianism is an offence to the questioning mind

This approach encourages us to use our minds to prove the existence of God, and to establish the supreme authority of the church which guarantees the truth of God's revelation. And once we have accepted this authority, everything else follows. We can ask questions about what the revelation means, and in certain matters there may be liberty in interpretation; but we cannot question the truth of the revelation.

In practice this kind of authoritarian approach has often led to:

either a blind and unquestioning acceptance of what the church teaches;

or a rebellion against the authoritative teaching of the church even among those who stay within the church, and a refusal to accept all its teachings;

or a total rejection of the church as an authoritative teacher of the truth;

or a mysticism which allows the individual to sit loosely to the accepted formulae of the church, and at the same time to remain within the church.

The following extracts are from writers who explain why they reject this kind of authoritarianism:

A Roman Catholic Modernist, writing in 1905:

The very idea of dogma is now repugnant, and a source of scandal.

These are the reasons he gives, as summarized by Alec Vidler:

1. A dogma appeared to be a proposition that was said to be intrinsically true, neither proved nor provable. But nowadays men rightly want to

RECOMMENDATION.

I Certify that the sacred Text of the New Testament, in this Edition of it, is conformable to that of former approved Editions; and particularly to that of the Douay English Version sanctioned by me, and published by R. Cross, in the year 1791.

✠ J. T. TROY, D.D. &c.

Dublin, 9th Feb. 1820.

Translation.

AN EXTRACT OF A RESCRIPT,

ADDRESSED BY HIS HOLINESS

PIUS VII.

TO THE

VICARS APOSTOLIC OF GREAT BRITAIN.

" VICARS APOSTOLIC labouring in the Vineyard of our Lord,

" Direct all your zeal and attention to this, that all the faithful whom we
" have committed to your pastoral care, love one another in Charity, Sincerity,
" and Truth : that in the present general agitation, they shew themselves an
" example of good works : that they obey the King, and be so dutiful and
" faithful to him, that our adversaries may fear, (not having it in their power)
" to speak ill of us ; that they abstain from reading vicious books, by which,
" in these most calamitous times, our holy religion is in all directions assailed ;
" that by reading pious books, *and above all the HOLY SCRIPTURES, in
' the Editions approved by the Church,* they conform in faith and good works
" to you, as their pattern in precept and practice. While we trust from your
" fidelity and proved veneration for us. that this duty shall be duly performed,
" we impart to you the Apostolic benediction.

" Given at Rome at the College of Holy Mary the Greater, on the 18th of
" April, Year of Grace, 1820, of our Pontificate, 21.

Dublin: Printed by Richard Coyne, 4 Capel-street, Printer and Bookseller to the Royal College of St. Patrick. Maynooth ; and Publisher to the Roman Catholic Bishops of Ireland.

be shown that there are reasonable grounds for belief.

2. If reasons for accepting dogmatic propositions are forthcoming, they take the form of an appeal to a transcendent authority that is supposed, as it were, to introduce the truth into us from outside. A dogma thus seems to be an external fetter, a limit to thought, a sort of intellectual tyranny, denying man's need to be autonomous and sincere.

3. Allowing for the sake of argument that dogmas could be simply taught by a doctrinal authority, they would in that case have to be intelligible and unambiguous. But the trouble with traditional Christian dogmas was that they were expressed in philosophical terminology. 'In short, the first difficulty which numbers of people today find when confronted with dogmas is that they do not convey to them any intelligible meaning. These statements say nothing to them, or rather seem to them to be indissolubly bound up with a state of mind which is no longer theirs . . Many believers are implicitly of the same opinion and so prefer to abstain from reflecting on their faith.'

4. There is the grave objection that dogmas do not cohere with the rest of knowledge. Dogmas too are supposed to be immutable while thought is always progressive. Dogmas do not throw any light on scientific or philosophical problems. They do not connect.

H. J. Blackham:

An open mind is vulnerable to evidence.

By comparison a religious faith may not be vulnerable. If the believer will not allow that any experience could falsify his belief, he does not have an open mind about it because it is not founded on rational grounds. His faith rests in something other than the reliability of tested evidence. His trust is likely to be in God, who is then at once the author and the object of the faith.

George Harrison:

When you're young you get taken to church by your parents and you get pushed into religion at school. They're trying to put something into your mind. But it's wrong you know. Obviously because nobody goes to church and nobody believes in God. Why? Because religious teachers don't know what they're teaching. They haven't interpreted the Bible as it was intended.

This is the thing that led me into the Indian scene, that I didn't really believe in God as I'd been taught it. It was just like something out of a

George Harrison of the Beatles.

science fiction novel . . . You're taught just to have faith, you don't have to worry about it, just believe what we're telling you.

Dostoievsky makes a vigorous protest against authoritarian Christianity and is very well aware of the connection between authoritarian religion and authoritarian government. In his imaginary account of the Grand Inquisitor, the Inquisitor represents the authoritarianism of the Roman Catholic Church at the time of the Inquisition in the sixteenth century. This is how the Inquisitor speaks to Christ when he meets him face to face:

Why . . . did you come to meddle with us? . . . Tomorrow I shall condemn you and burn you at the stake as the vilest of heretics . . . Have you the right to reveal to us even one of the mysteries of the world you have come from? . . . No, you have not. So that you may not add anything to what has been said before and so as not to deprive men of the freedom which you upheld so strongly when you were here on earth. All that you might reveal anew would encroach on men's freedom of faith, for it would come as a miracle, and their freedom of faith was dearer to you than anything even in those days, fifteen hundred years ago. Was it not you who said so often in those days, 'I shall make you free'? But now you have seen those 'free' men . . . Yes, this business has cost us a great deal . . . but we've completed it at last in your name. For fifteen centuries we've been troubled by this freedom, but now it's over and done with for good . . . These men are more than ever convinced that they are absolutely free, and yet they themselves have brought their freedom to us and humbly laid it at our feet . . .

You did not come down from the cross when they shouted to you, mocking and deriding you: 'If you be the Son of God, come down from the cross.' You did not come down because . . . you did not want to enslave man by miracles and because you hungered for a faith based on free will and not on miracles. You hungered for freely given love and not for the servile rapture of the slave before the might that has terrified him once and for all . . .

There is a mystery here and we cannot understand it. And if it is a mystery, then we, too, were entitled to preach a mystery and to teach them that it is neither the free verdict of their hearts nor that love that matters, but the mystery which they must obey blindly, even against their own consciences. So we have done. We have corrected your great work and have based it on *miracle*, *mystery*, and *authority*. And men rejoiced that they were once more led like sheep and that the terrible gift which had brought them so much suffering had at last been lifted from their hearts . . . Why, then, have you come to meddle with us now? And why are you looking at me silently and so penetratingly with your gentle eyes?

Authoritarianism, however, is not by any means confined to one church, and it is not necessarily associated with the view that some truths can be proved by reason. Sometimes those who regard the Bible as the supreme authority (*i.e.* they believe the first part of answer 1, pp. 12–30) use the authority of the Bible in the same way as the Catholic uses the authority of church. They make frequent use of the phrase 'the Bible says . . .', usually with the implication 'what the Bible says must, by definition, be true; and you have no alternative but to accept what it says'.

Emil Brunner links together these two approaches in this way:

From the outset it is assumed that the Christian Faith is the true Faith, because this faith is taught either in the Bible or by the Church. But the fact that the doctrine of the Church, or of the Bible, is 'the truth', must be accepted as axiomatic. We believe in Jesus Christ, because we believe first of all either in the doctrinal authority of the Church, or in that of the Bible.

The resulting dilemma is well expressed by this *cri de coeur* written by the 24-year-old daughter of missionary parents:

I have been taught the Christian faith from childhood. I attended a Christian high school and college. According to the accepted pattern I should now be a stable, vibrant Christian . . . I wish I could conform to that pattern. But I cannot . . . I grew up praying, attending church, reading my Bible, witnessing and giving testimonies . . .

Then came a series of events that stopped me cold. I began to wonder if I really owned all that I claimed. I started to ask the meaning of faith in Christ, salvation by grace, and many other phrases that I had tossed around all my life . . . Realizing my faith was not truly my own, I then refused to give intellectual assent to forms of belief that I did not feel within myself. I could no longer accept without examination that which is supposed to meet man's deepest needs.

As I now stand facing adulthood, I am overwhelmed by the incomprehensibility of life. I often see myself as an unwelcome guest in a seemingly impersonal, deterministic universe. And I ask 'Why am I here anyway?' I am like many other twentieth-century young people whose 'blazing optimism' is tainted and dulled by fear.

I long to know God through an intimate relationship with Jesus Christ. I have gone through the act of accepting Christ as my personal Saviour, but how can he meet my deepest needs? The simple statement of 'Just trust the Lord' does not satisfy my intellectual restlessness nor my emotional turmoil. Such statements and phrases I have heard so often that they are trite and meaningless in the complexity of my individual context. I cannot accept 'pat' answers, for to me they are dead clichés and platitudes that do not meet my feelings . . .

Occasionally I have suggested to my parents and evangelical friends that I must have opportunity to think and discover for my own satisfaction the form of faith that is to satisfy me. My parents accuse me of 'going away from the Lord', of backsliding. They say my thinking is dangerous to my spiritual life. Perhaps so, but is it any less dangerous to be a robot responding to mechanical instructions?

I am putting this down on paper because I have found that I am not alone in the struggle. Others are searching, too, for a personal and satisfying relationship with God. I have talked with many other young people who have a deep desire for meaningful communication with Jesus Christ, though they have known 'the answers' all their lives. We wonder how can parents and other adults help us?

I believe you can help by giving us sympathy and understanding ... Most young people in this situation are in the process of trying to discover themselves as well, and we tend to rebel against any ideas that seem to be offered to us as a substitute for our thinking for ourselves ... Even quoting Scripture to us can be infuriating, because usually we are just as aware of these verses as you are, and we tend to wonder if they actually meet your needs any more than they meet ours ... Your concern for me as an individual will have far deeper effects than if you try to offer answers ... Parents will do well to try to understand the effects that modern psychological pressures have on the emotions of youth and why we are reacting in this manner, instead of throwing up their hands in horror at the attitudes we express. Patiently encourage us and give us the freedom to search for a meaningful relationship to God and to find a real expression for that relationship.

Muslims in the past have assumed that the Qur'an is the word of God. The impact of modern ways of thinking, however, is likely to make more and more people ask the question, 'How can I *know* if the Qur'an is the word of God?'

Wilfred Cantwell Smith:

Muslims do not read the Qur'an and conclude that it is divine; rather, they believe that it is divine, and then they read it.

The Muslim world, also, is moving into what may possibly become a profound crisis, too; in that it also is just beginning to ask this question, instead of being content only with answering it. Young people in Lahore and Cairo, labour leaders in Jakarta and Istanbul, are beginning to ask their religious thinkers, and beginning to ask themselves, 'Is the Qur'an the word of God?' Answering this question has been the business of the Muslim world for over thirteen centuries. Asking it is a different matter altogether, haunting and ominous.

When these questions are asked, the authoritarianism of Islam leads in practice to the same kind of reactions as the authoritarianism of Roman Catholicism:

either a blind and unquestioning acceptance of the Qur'an;

or an intellectual scepticism about God, combined with a limited practice of the Muslim way of life;

or a total rejection of Islamic beliefs about God and the supernatural;

or a mysticism which enables the Muslim to bypass or transcend certain intellectual problems.

3. THE ANSWER OF RATIONALISM AND ROMANTICISM

"Christian beliefs are true only if they accord with human reason and/or feeling"

Rationalism and Romanticism both hold that Christian beliefs can only be accepted as true if they accord with reason and/or the heart. This answer varies according to where the emphasis is placed:

☐ **Man can find the truth through his reason alone; there is no need for any revelation from God;**

☐ **Man can find the truth through reason and the heart.**

MAN CAN FIND THE TRUTH THROUGH HIS REASON ALONE

It is important to stress that most of the philosophers who thought in this way were *not atheists*. They did not deny the existence of God. They simply said that God had little or nothing to do with man's search after the truth.

Ernst Cassirer says that in the early Italian Renaissance there were three major currents of philosophical thought: Humanism (which was largely interested in classical studies, and was not opposed to Christianity or the church), Platonism, and Aristotelianism (which looked to Averroes as a guide, and eventually came to inspire the free-thinkers of the seventeenth century, especially in France). The following are some of the ideas of this third group:

The supremacy of natural reason, the denial of creation and personal immortality, with their theological consequences, and the unity of the intellect were taught in the universities and, we are told, accepted by many Venetian gentlemen. Such a philosophy expressed with precision the stage of scepticism towards the religious system, of anti-supernaturalism rather than of positive naturalism and humanism, which had been reached by the northern Italian cities in the fourteenth century.

Paul Hazard describes the more advanced stage reached by the end of the seventeenth century:

What men craved to know was what they were to believe, and what they were not to believe. Was tradition still to command their allegiance, or was it to go by the board? Were they to continue plodding along the same old road, trusting to the same old guides, or were they to obey new leaders who bade them turn their back on all those outworn things and follow them to other lands of promise. The champions of Reason and the champions of Religion were . . . fighting desperately for the possession of men's souls, confronting each other in a contest at which the whole of thoughtful Europe was looking on.

He describes the attitudes of the seventeenth- and eighteenth-century Rationalists in this way:

And now Reason breaks loose and there's no holding her any longer. Tradition, authority are nothing to her; 'What harm,' she says, 'in wiping the slate clean and beginning things all over again?' . . . Heaven was theirs, and earth was theirs; theirs was the whole domain of the know-able. There was nothing, they thought, nothing in the whole universe which the geometrical mind could not grasp. Theology, too, was their business . . .

Descartes the geometrician had called the tune for the new era. But what if the geometrical mind collides head on with religion? What will happen if it is applied wholesale to matters of faith? It would mean putting the sponge over the religious slate; every religion would be wiped out.

Hazard traces the connection between the seventeenth century and the Renaissance in this way:

This critical urge, whence came it? Who fostered it? What made it at once so daring and so strong? Where, in a word, did it originate? The answer is that it came from afar, from very far indeed: it came from ancient Greece; from this, that, or another heretical doctor of the Middle Ages; from many other distant sources, but beyond all doubt or question it came from the Renaissance. Between the Renaissance and the period we have just been studying (*i.e.* 1680–1715), the family-likeness is unmistakable. There is the same refusal on the part of the more daring spirits to subordinate the human to the divine. In both cases a like importance is assigned to man, to man who has no rival, man who limits the boundary of the knowable, resolves all problems that admit of solution, regarding the rest as null and void, man the source and centre of the hopes of the world. Now and then, Nature comes in, not very clearly defined, but powerful, Nature no longer regarded as the work of a Creator, but as the upsurge of life as a whole, and of human life in particular . . . This age bears upon it all the characteristics of a second Renaissance but a Renaissance sterner, more austere, and, in a measure, disillusioned, a Renaissance without a Rabelais, a Renaissance without a smile . . .

And so the trend of modern thought can be charted more or less accurately as follows: starting from the Renaissance, an eagerness for invention, a passion for discovery, an urge to play the critic, traits all so manifest that we may call them the dominant elements in the European mentality. Somewhere about the middle of the seventeenth century there was a temporary pause, when a truce, wholly unlooked for, was entered into by the opposing forces, an entirely unpredictable reconciliation. This phenomenon, which was nothing short of miraculous, was what is called the Revival of Learning, the revival of the classical spirit, and the fruit of it was peace and tranquil strength . . .

As soon as the classical ideal ceased to be a thing to aim at, a deliberated goal, a conscious choice, and began to degenerate into a mere habit, and an irksome one at that, the innovators, all ready for action, set to work with all the old zest and energy. And so, yet once again, the mind of Europe set out on the unending quest. Then came a crisis so swift and so sudden, so at least it seemed, that it took men completely by surprise; yet it had long been stirring in the womb of Time, and, so far from being a new thing, was in reality a very old one.

Two formative thinkers

René Descartes (1596–1650):

▷ His basic principle was that of systematic doubt:

My first rule was to accept nothing as true which I did not clearly recognize to be so; to accept nothing more than what was presented to my mind so clearly and distinctly that I could have no occasion to doubt it.

▷ One thing, however, which he could not doubt was his own existence:

Cogito, ergo sum. I think, therefore I am.

▷ He was also aware that he was finite. And if he was finite, this implied that there must be an infinite Being. He himself was aware that he was imperfect, and this awareness implied that a perfect Being must exist.

It is inconceivable that God should deceive us by giving us ideas of this kind if they are not true. Therefore God must exist.

John Locke (1632–1704):

The following are the basic ideas of his philosophy which are relevant here:

▷ The mind is like a blank piece of paper which receives all its impressions from outside. It is like 'white paper void of all characters, without any ideas'.

In bare naked perception the mind is, for the most part, merely passive.

▷ All human knowledge is either '*ideas*' (which are impressions on the mind from external objects—such as yellow, white, heat, cold, soft, hard, bitter, sweet, and all those which we call sensible qualities) or the *reflection* of the mind on these ideas.

Human knowledge therefore hath no other immediate object but its own ideas.

▷ Reason and faith are totally different:

Reason is the discovery of the certainty or probability of such propositions or truths, which the mind arrives at by deduction made from such *ideas*, which it has got by the use of its natural faculties, *viz.* by sensation or reflection.

Faith, on the other hand, is the assent to any proposition not thus made out by the deductions of reason, but upon the credit of the proposer, as coming from God, in some extraordinary way of communication. This way of discovering truths to men we call *Revelation*.

As an example of a truth of reason, he gives the existence of God.

The works of nature everywhere sufficiently evidence a Deity.

The existence of God is 'the most obvious truth that reason discovers'; 'its evidence,' he says, is 'equal to mathematical certainty.'

Any truth of revelation must be tested by truths of reason. If it does not contradict what we know by reason, then it can be accepted. But if it does, it must be rejected.

Revelation is natural *reason* enlarged by a new set of discoveries communicated by God immediately, which *reason* vouches the truth of by the testimony and proofs that they come from God.

No principle can be received for divine revelation, or obtain the assent due to such, if it be contrary to our clear intuitive knowledge.

This is how *Paul Hazard* describes the revolutionary impact of Locke's philosophy:

Locke it was who turned the attention of thinkers to psychological truths, truths present in the mind, living, constant, and indefectible . . .

An Essay concerning Human Understanding. Whatever may be said of it by those who care only for the high flights of philosophy, the date marks a definite change, a new orientation. Henceforth man's sphere of exploration was the mind of man and its unfathomable riches. Let us have done, said Locke, with these metaphysical conjectures; do we not realize how fruitless they are? Are we not tired of asking and always asking in vain? . . .
The certitude which we need resides in the mind. Let us look therein and cease to probe those infinite spaces which do but breed deceiving visions; thereon let us concentrate our attention. Clearly recognizing that our understanding is limited, let us accept its limitations . . . Putting aside the hope of attaining any perfect and absolute knowledge of the things around us as something beyond the range of finite beings, let us content ourselves with being what we are, with doing what we can, and with knowing what we can know.

This is *G. R. Cragg's* estimate of his influence:

John Locke epitomized the intellectual outlook of his own age and shaped that of the next. For over a century he dominated European thought . . . The spirit in which he dealt with Christianity is more important than what he actually said about it. He made a certain attitude to religious faith almost universal.

The influence of ideas of this kind are clearly seen in the *American Declaration of Independence* of 1776:

We hold these truths to be self-evident, that all men are created equal, and that they are endowed by their Creator with certain inalienable rights . . .

MAN CAN FIND THE TRUTH THROUGH REASON AND THE HEART

As men became conscious of the one-sided emphasis on reason in the eighteenth century, or as they became aware of the inability of reason to find convincing answers by itself they began to feel that truth must be sought through reason *and* the heart working together.

By the 1760s the scientific and philosophical speculation of the Enlightenment seemed to have ended in an impasse. Chance, or the blind determinism of matter in regular but aimless motion, appeared to regulate the operations of the universe and the destiny of man. If metaphysical speculation had any meaning at all—which the sceptics denied— it served merely to open a window on to the blank wall of necessity. A brilliant and inquisitive age was not likely to be content for long with such a prospect, and in response to the challenge new attitudes were evolved that transformed the terms in which men thought of themselves and of the order of the universe. One of the most significant of these attitudes . . . was the acceptance of the heart as legitimate consort of the head. It is important . . . to realize what this new assumption did *not* imply. To present it as a revolt against an age of arid intellectualism seems to me to betray extraordinary insensitivity towards the vigour of eighteenth-century life and the excitement of its speculative thought. What happened was not that the artist usurped the position formerly occupied by the scholar, but that both turned to the emotions for the guidance they had previously expected of their reason. Sentiment came to be accepted as the source of a kind of knowledge to which intelligence could not aspire, and as the arbiter of action. But if feeling became pilot, reason remained in command, except for a few extremists whose shipwreck discouraged imitation. The definition of their respective roles could never be established with finality but there was no question of the elimination of reason. However dramatically this new attitude may have seemed to challenge the urbanity of the Enlightenment, both grew from a common stock and both were rooted in the same intellectual soil . . .

In so far as one can ascribe a definite starting-point to a change in attitude, the most appropriate date would be 1749, when Rousseau wrote his prize essay on the subject set by the Dijon Academy: *Whether the restoration of the arts and sciences has contributed to the refinement of morals.* In other words, the 'reaction' against the Enlightenment preceded most of the major works of the Enlightenment itself! (Hampson)

Two formative thinkers

Jean Jacques Rousseau (1712–1778):

As the eighteenth century wore on, it was discovered that the 'Nature' of man was not his 'reason' at all, but his instincts, emotions, and 'sensibilities', and what was more, people began to glory in this discovery, and to regard reason itself as an aberration from 'Nature'. *Cogito ergo sum* is superseded by *je sens, donc je suis* associated with Rousseau. Shaftesbury, Hutcheson, and Hume had prepared the way by proclaiming that our moral judgements, like our aesthetic judgements, are not the offspring of Reason at all but proceed from an inner sentiment or feeling which is unanalysable. (Basil Willey)

He stressed the part played by the emotions, not only in religion, but in literature, politics, and philosophy. He offered a broad and original treatment of all fields on the basis of his new sensibility. The result to a large extent of his work was the so-called Romantic Movement. This is the essential content of Rousseau, the 'outsider,' who fathered the romantic sensibility and opposed it to the dominant rationalism of his time. (Bronowski and Mazlish)

S. T. Coleridge (1772–1834):

Coleridge was well aware of the challenge to Christian faith from the philosophers Hume and Kant. His response was to emphasize the difference between reason and faith, and to associate faith with the conscience, or moral consciousness. In this way he made faith immune from refutation by reason. Faith cannot be proved rationally, and even if it could it would produce a compulsory assent.

Yet there had dawned upon me, even before I had met with the *Critique of Pure Reason*, a certain guiding light. If the mere intellect could make no certain discovery of a holy and intelligent first cause, it might yet supply a demonstration, that no legitimate argument could be drawn from the intellect *against* its truth. And what is this more than St Paul's assertion that by wisdom (more perfectly translated by the powers of reasoning) no man ever arrived at the knowledge of God? . . . I became convinced that religion as both the corner-stone and the key-stone of morality, must have a *moral* origin; so far at least, that the evidence of its doctrines could not, like the truths of abstract science, be wholly independent of the will. It was therefore to be expected, that its *fundamental* truth would be such as *might* be denied; though only by the fool, and even by the fool from the madness of the heart alone.

This kind of answer, with the stress on reason or feeling or on both together, is still expressed today:

James Thurber:

It may be that the finer mysteries of life and death can be comprehended only through pure instinct; the cat, for example, appears to Know (I don't say that he does, but he appears to). Man, on the other hand, is surely farther away from the Answer than any other animal this side of the ladybug. His mistaken selection of reasoning as an instrument of perception has put him into a fine quandary.

H. J. Blackham:

. . . there is no immemorial tradition, no revelation, no authority, no privileged knowledge (first principles, intuitions, axioms) which is beyond question because beyond experience and which can be used as a standard by which to interpret experience. There is only experience to be interpreted in the light of further experience, the sole

"Dogs suffer from depression" . . . One of James Thurber's illustrations from Vintage Thurber.

source of all standards of reason and value, for ever open to question.

Humanism is rooted in two historical quests of universal import: free inquiry and social agreement.

PROBLEMS AND QUESTIONS

Man's reason becomes the ultimate arbiter

Man starts with the assumptions which his reason approves, and if a so-called revelation does not fit in with these assumptions, so much the worse for the revelation. This subordination is seen, e.g. in Locke and Newton.

Locke's strong emphasis on reason naturally raised the question of the status of revelation. He did not doubt its reality or its importance, but he reinterpreted it in conformity with his general picture of the religious life. What revelation confirms is the essentially reasonable character of Christianity. It shows that few dogmas are necessary; they are simple, and intelligible to ordinary men. Christianity has one essential doctrine: Jesus is the Messiah. Locke thus carried simplification to its extreme limits; most of the structure of traditional theology was casually dismissed as irrelevant. (G. R. Cragg)

Sir Isaac Newton had of course no intention of repudiating Christianity; he merely proposed to reinterpret its truths, but his rationalistic restatement left few of its traditional doctrines untouched. (G. R. Cragg)

Locke's approach determined the main thrust of Christian apologetics during the following century:

The title of Locke's treatise, *The Reasonableness of Christianity*, may be said to have been the solitary thesis of Christian theology in England for the greater part of a century. (Mark Pattison)

The very titles of the main works of the period indicate the extent to which the Christian revelation was subordinated to Reason:

> *Christianity Not Mysterious, Showing that there is Nothing in the Gospel contrary to Reason nor above it, and that no Christian Doctrine can properly be called a Mystery*, by John Toland, 1696.

> *Christianity as Old as the Creation; or, the Gospel a Republication of the Religion of Nature*, by Matthew Tindal, 1730.

> *The Analogy of Religion, Natural and Revealed, to the Constitution and Course of Nature*, by Joseph Butler, 1736.

Butler's work is the high-water mark of this approach. He argues that Nature is full of mysteries and obscurities; and 'Probability' is the best guide in life. If this is the case in the 'natural' world, he says, surely we should be prepared to expect the same mysteries and obscurities and probabilities in what claims to be a 'supernatural' revelation.

Towards the close of the seventeenth century the prestige of Scripture, though outwardly unchanged, had actually diminished appreciably. It was not so much that men had rejected it as 'false'; it was rather that as 'natural religion' came more and more to seem all-sufficient, 'revelation' began to appear, if not superfluous, at least secondary, and perhaps even slightly inconvenient. An age which discovered God effortlessly in the starry heavens above, and in the moral law within, could not but be embarrassed by having to acknowledge dependence upon the annals and legends of an unenlightened Semitic tribe . . . By the time we reach Joseph Butler, Nature, instead of being a valuable supplement to Revelation as it was with Bacon, has virtually become the standard against which Revelation itself is to be tested. (Basil Willey)

Tertullian of old could say *credo quia impossibile*; now an eighteenth-century saint asks us to believe Revelation to be authentic *because* it is as bewildering as an admittedly divine Nature. In this paradoxical defence Butler may seem to have virtually wiped out the distinction between Revelation and Nature. (Basil Willey)

 ## Christian beliefs are whittled down

If revelation is completely subordinate to reason, then reason must be free to reject any Christian beliefs which it finds to be unreasonable or offensive.

▷ *Locke* reduced the essential content of the Christian faith to faith in Christ, and in the doctrine of repentance; the only condition of salvation, belief in the mission of Jesus, and living a good life.

▷ *Friedrich Schleiermacher*, the German theologian (1768–1834) reduced the essence of Christianity to 'a feeling of absolute dependence'.

▷ *Adolph von Harnack*, the German theologian (1851–1930) reduced the essence of the teaching of Jesus to these three themes: the Kingdom of God and its coming; God the Father and the infinite value of the human soul; the higher righteousness and the commandment of love.

▷ *D. F. Strauss* in his *Life of Jesus* (written in 1835–36) entirely denied the supernatural element in the Gospels:

All things are linked together by a chain of causes and effects, which suffers no interruption . . . This conviction is so much a habit of thought with the modern world, that in actual life, the belief in a supernatural manifestation, an immediate divine agency, is at once attributed to ignorance or imposture.

In the person and acts of Jesus no supernaturalism shall be allowed to remain. He who would banish priests from the Church must first banish miracles from religion.

Scepticism – the logical conclusion

What happens when 'Reason' and 'Nature' are unable to point unambiguously to the truth? What happens when the heart and the mind give very different answers?

The famous eighteenth-century alliance between Nature and Reason had begun to crumble; Reason, it was found, could lead one way, and Nature another. Or, putting it another way, the 'Nature' to which the century had so confidently appealed could have two main sets of meanings: it could mean the head. or it could mean the heart; ideas or facts; theories or history; what is congenial to abstract reason, or what is dear to the heart. The nineteenth century went on believing in 'Nature', but not without misgivings due to the inherent contradictions of the creed. Was Nature best expressed in the 'march of the mind', or in the heart's affections . . . These, it was found, could conflict. (Basil Willey)

The logical conclusion to which this answer pointed, therefore, was a position of complete scepticism. Having denied certain beliefs of Christianity, the critic begins to feel 'Why stop here? Why reject this, but accept that?' But many who saw that their questioning should lead them to a position of total doubt were unwilling to be utterly consistent.

This is how Paul Hazard describes the position of *Pierre Bayle,* one of the most radical of the French free-thinkers (1647–1706):

Did he reach the point of absolute scepticism? He would have done so had he suffered his mind to follow its natural bent. Nothing ever pleased him better than that interplay of *pro* and *con*. He would have floated away into that far-off void, where actions lose their significance and life its purpose, had he followed logic to its final term, and taken cognizance only of his human experience, which day by day impressed him more and more. He might, nay, he must, have arrived at last at what Le Clerc calls metaphysical and historical scepticism, at universal doubt.

But this he resisted. His intrepid spirit, the feeling that he had a mission to fulfil, an abhorrence of error, more potent than any doubt he might have entertained about truth, a reasoning mind that would not willingly accept defeat, and above all his strength of will enabled him to stop short of the final step.

The most advanced unbelievers among the thinkers with whom we have been dealing called a halt when they came face to face with the Nihilism to which their scepticism seemed about to lead them.

The irrational leap of faith

Some found it possible to hold on to some form of Christian beliefs by taking a leap of faith. Having already accepted that Christian faith is in a different category from all that is investigated by the reason, it was not hard for them to feel that it was immune from the questioning of the reason.

Coleridge, for example, made a distinction between the 'understanding' (*i.e.* the intellect, the mind) and what he called 'the reason' (meaning by it an inward intuitive faculty, not the intellect). This distinction enabled him to feel that his faith was not vulnerable to the challenges of reason. But there were others like *Thomas Carlyle* who pointed out the irrationality which seemed to be implied in this approach:

What the light of your mind, which is the direct inspiration of the Almighty, pronounces incredible,—that, in God's name, leave uncredited; at your peril do not try believing that. No subtlest hocus-pocus of 'reason' *versus* 'understanding' will avail for that feat . . .!

To *steal* into heaven, by the modern method, of sticking ostrich-like your head into fallacies on Earth, . . . is forever forbidden. High treason is the name of that attempt . . .

What can it profit any mortal to adopt locutions and imaginations which do *not* correspond to fact; which no sane mortal can deliberately adopt in his soul as true; which the most orthodox of mortals can only, and this after infinite essentially *impious* effort to put out the eyes of his mind, persuade himself to 'believe that he believes'? Away with it; in the name of God, come out of it, all true men!

4. THE ANSWER OF AGNOSTICISM

"We can never know for certain whether or not Christianity is true"

The agnostic says: no matter how hard we try to find the truth through reason or the heart, we cannot hope to find it. Our minds are finite, and we cannot solve the mysteries of the universe. We must be content to recognize the limits of our knowledge, and not hope to know anything beyond these limits.

SOME TWENTIETH-CENTURY EXAMPLES

A. J. Ayer:

While I believe that there can be an explanation in mundane terms for anything that happens within the world, I do not think it makes sense to ask for an explanation of the existence or the characteristics of the world as a whole. In this sense, it is a matter of brute fact that the universe exhibits the patterns which it does.

Aldous Huxley:

The only facts of which we have direct knowledge are psychological facts. The Nature of Things presents us with them. There is no getting round them, or behind them, or outside of them. They are there, given.

One fact cannot be more of a fact than another. Our psychological experiences are all equally facts. There is nothing to chose between them. No psychological experience is 'truer', so far as we are concerned, than any other. For even if one should correspond more closely to things in themselves as perceived by some hypothetical non-human being, it would be impossible for us to discover what it was.

No man has a right to speak for any one except himself and those who happen to resemble him . . . Every man has as good a right to his own particular world-view as to his own particular kidneys . . .

I have no desire to impose my particular brand of life-worship on any one else . . . We admit that every man has a right in these matters to his own tastes. 'I like lobsters; you don't. And there's an end of it.' Such is the argument of gastronomers. In time, perhaps, philosophers will learn to treat one another with the same politeness and forbearance.

The life-worshipper's philosophy is comprehensive. As a manifold and discontinuous being, he is in a position to accept all the partial and apparently contradictory syntheses constructed by other philosophers . . . Each belief is the rationalization of the prevailing mood . . . There is really no question of any of these philosophies being true or false . . . And since one psychological state cannot be truer than another, since all are equally facts, it follows that the rationalization of one state cannot be truer than the rationalization of another . . . The only branches of philosophy in regard to which it is permissible to talk of truth and falsehood are logic and the theory of knowledge.

Jacquetta Hawkes:

In all this realm of ultimate meaning there is only one thing I believe with certainty – that we live in an impenetrable mystery. The more that we find out about the Universe, the greater this mystery becomes. Our discoveries inspire us with unending wonder, but not with final understanding.

Rebecca West:

I have no faith in the sense of comforting beliefs which persuade me that all my troubles are blessings in disguise. I do not believe that any facts exist, or, rather, are accessible to me, which give any assurance that my life has served an eternal purpose.

Albert Einstein:

To ponder interminably over the reason for one's own existence or the meaning of life in general seems to me, from an objective point of view, to be sheer folly.

Barbara Wooton:

The universe in general must, I think, simply be accepted as a totally inexplicable mystery.

H. J. Blackham:

Scientific enquiry presupposes the situation of human beings confronting objects in this world. Anything supposed outside these conditions is not open to its inquiry. Anything totally transcendent, encompassing both subject and object, for example, is beyond such enquiry, and beyond conceptual thought ... Ultimately, everything as given is equally inscrutable and mysterious; there is nothing privileged in terms of which all the rest can be explained. This is what is meant by the renunciation of 'God-like knowledge'. A-gnosticism, which is more fundamental and radical than atheism, is the only position warranted by experience: recognition of the permanent nature and conditions of human knowledge, with its open horizon of continuous progressive investigation.

THREE FORMATIVE THINKERS

David Hume (1711-1776)

The basic points in his philosophy which concern us are these:

▷ We perceive the data of our senses; and we cannot hope to go beyond our senses or to know anything beyond what they tell us.

Let us fix our attention out of ourselves as much as possible: let us chase our imagination to the heavens, or to the utmost limits of the universe; we never really advance a step beyond ourselves, nor can we conceive any kind of existence, but those perceptions, which have appear'd in that narrow compass. This is the universe of the imagination, nor have we any idea by what is there produc'd.

▷ The idea that every like cause produces a like effect is a product of our own thinking. It cannot be inferred from the data of our senses. If cause *a* always seems to produce effect *b*, we have no justification for saying that *a* has *caused b*, it is only habit or custom which makes us think that this is so. All that we are entitled to say is that *a* generally seems to be followed by *b*.

There is nothing in any object, considered by itself, which can afford us a reason for drawing a conclusion beyond it.

'Tis not, therefore, reason, which is the guide of life, but custom. That alone determines the mind, in all instances, to suppose the future conformable to the past. However easy this step may seem, reason would never, to all eternity, be able to make it.

▷ Hume also held that the idea of miracles violates the principle of the uniformity of natural causes, and must therefore be ruled out as impossible.

Immanuel Kant (1724-1804)

The following are the main points of his philosophy which concern us here:

▷ He agreed with Hume and the empiricists in saying that 'all knowledge begins with experience'. He acknowledged his debt to Hume and said that it was the reading of his works which awoke him from his dogmatic slumbers.

▷ But at the same time, 'it does not follow that it all arises out of experience.' The mind also plays a part, and is therefore not a complete *tabula rasa*. In this he disagrees with Locke. The mind does not perceive things precisely as they are: it conditions everything it perceives.

▷ He then asks: if this is the case, what are the proper limits of human thought and knowledge? And his answer is to make a distinction between *knowledge* which has to do with *phenomena* (everything that can be seen) and *faith* which has to do with *noumena* (truths beyond space and time). These are two completely different ways of knowing, and they are another example of the dichotomy which we have already seen in Locke and others (compare the diagram on p. 35):

FAITH

――――――――

KNOWLEDGE

Faith is concerned with *noumena* above the line, truths beyond space and time, things 'in themselves', reality as it is, the truths of religion (such as the existence of God, free will, immortality). Knowledge, *phenomena*, is truth which can be perceived by the senses, *i.e.* through science, truth about the external world of space and time.

Because of this distinction, therefore, we must accept the fact that we cannot *know* anything for certain beyond our direct experience of this world. Religious beliefs have their origin in the moral consciousness, but they cannot be classed as knowledge. This limitation of knowledge ensures the possibility of religious faith, because it makes it impervious to the attacks of sceptics.

I have therefore found it necessary to deny *knowledge* to make room for *faith*.

George Frederick Hegel (1770-1831)

▷ Hegel accepted Kant's distinction between faith and knowledge.

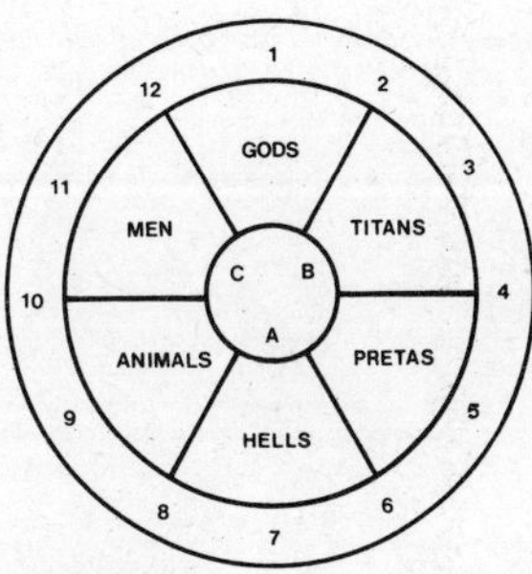

A *Delusion*
B *Greed*
C *Hatred*
1 *Blind woman: ignorance*
2 *Potter: karmic formations*
3 *Monkey: consciousness*
4 *Two men in a boat: mind-and-body*
5 *House with six windows: six senses*
6 *Pair of lovers: contact*
7 *Arrow piercing eye of man: feeling*
8 *Drinker, served by woman: thirst*
9 *Man gathering fruit: clinging*
10 *Sexual intercourse: becoming*
11 *Woman giving birth: birth*
12 *Man carrying corpse: death*

Tibetan 'Wheel of Life', from a Tibetan temple—fresco of Sankar Gompa, Leh.

▷ He thought of truth as the 'synthesis of opposing viewpoints'. Nothing is true in any absolute sense. All that we can expect is that one idea (*thesis*) will be challenged by an opposite idea (*antithesis*), and that this will in turn be superseded by an idea which transcends the two contradictory ideas (*synthesis*). This means that in discussions about truth, the basic rule of logic no longer applies. For in the dialectical process, views which are mutually incompatible can be held together.

HINDUISM AND BUDDHISM

Both Hinduism and Buddhism are based on a profound agnosticism.

W. Cantwell Smith:

Hindus are so cheerfully diverse, so insistent that religious ways are many, that only vast and distorting oversimplification could predicate that their diversity and their ways is (I say 'ways is' to enforce my point) true or false. No Hindu has said anything that some other Hindu has not contradicted.

Radhakrishnan, writing about Hinduism:

While it gives absolute liberty in the world of thought, it injoins a strict code of practice. The theist, the sceptic and the agnostic may all be Hindus if they accept the Hindu system of culture and life . . . what counts is conduct, not belief.

K. M. Sen:

The religious beliefs of different schools of Hindu thought vary and their religious practices also differ; there is in it monism, dualism, monotheism, polytheism, pantheism, and indeed Hinduism is a great storehouse of all kinds of religious experiments.

Christmas Humphreys, writing about Buddhism:

The antitheses of cause and effect, substance and attribute, good and evil, truth and error, are due to the tendency of man to separate terms which are related. Fichte's puzzle of self and not-self, Kant's antinomies, and Hume's opposition of facts and laws, can all be got over if we recognize that the opposing factors are mutually complementary elements based on one identity!

PROBLEMS AND QUESTIONS

The laws of logic can be set aside

It is no longer necessary to say that *a* cannot be *non-a*. There need be no ideas which are incompatible. They can somehow be reconciled with each other and held together in such a way that they are both held to be true.

Leopold Senghor underlines the fundamental difference which Hegel's philosophy created:

What, then, is dialectics? . . . Today, we define dialectics by opposing it to logic. Classical logic rests on three principles: identity (A is A); non-contradiction (A is not non-A); and exclusion (A cannot be A and not be A at the same time). Hegel, with Marx following in his footsteps, opposes these principles, and proposes in their stead the principles of dialectics, which are: contradiction, reciprocal action, and change. For Hegel, the dialectical process is composed of three steps: affirmation, negation, and conciliation. For Marx, it consists of 'position, opposition, composition . . . We have thesis, antithesis, and synthesis . . . (or) affirmation, negation, and negation of the negation'. But that is only the beginning. The synthesis or 'new idea' is developed 'in two contradictory thoughts that blend in turn into a new synthesis' or 'groups of thoughts'. This group, continuing the process and developing into two groups of contradictory thoughts, ends in a 'series of thoughts'. The entire series of ideas forms the 'system' or body of doctrine.

In classical philosophy, which used logic, things and their concepts are objective realities placed one beside the other without any link or communication, fixed once and for all, immutable essences. They oppose each other in irreducible antitheses. Modern philosophy is quite different, for dialectics is its favourite instrument.

The dialectician can say at the same time: 'A is A' and 'A is not A', or 'A is not B' and 'A is B'.

Bronowski believes that when we are speaking about the meaning of human existence, we are in the realm of poetry, and in this realm there is no place for logic:

If logic asserts the proposition *P*, then it denies the proposition *not-P*. We are free in logic to say, if we believe it true, that love is simple, or blissful, or carnal; but we cannot then logically say of the same love that it is complex, or anguished, or spiritual. Even if we have a more sophisticated logic, in which there is a third alternative to *P* and *not-P*, that alternative asserts that they are both meaningless. But in poetry, to assert *P* and *not-P* together is not meaningless: it is not meaningless to say that love is ordinary and extraordinary at the same time. On the contrary, poetry claims that it contains the very meaning of the experience of living.

Aldous Huxley's agnosticism leads him to believe that God can be both one and many; both monotheism and polytheism can be true.

One psychological fact is as good as another; there is no conceivable method of demonstrating that God is either one or many. So far as human beings are concerned, he is both; monotheism and polytheism are equally true. But are they equally useful? Do they tend to the quickening and enhancement of human life?

Monotheism and polytheism are doctrines equally necessary and equally true. Man can and does conceive of himself and of the world as being, now essentially many, and now essentially one. Therefore – since God, for our human purposes, is simply Life in so far as men can conceive it as a whole – the Divine is both one and many. A purely monotheistic religion is thus seen to be inadequate and unrealistic.

When this procedure is carried over into theology, there are no longer any of the same distinctions or contradictions.

Paul Tillich believes that all religions must be subject to two ultimate criteria of religion:

. . . the criterion of a faith which transcends every finite symbol of faith and the criterion of a love which unconditionally affirms, judges and receives the other person.

Eastern wisdom, like every other wisdom, certainly belongs to the self-manifestation of the Logos and must be included in the interpretation of Jesus as the Christ, if he is rightly to be called the incarnation of the Logos.

Teilhard de Chardin:

As I like to say, the synthesis of the Christian 'God' on high and the Marxist 'God' of the future is the only God we can henceforth adore in spirit and in truth.

John Robinson:

There is a powerful and perennial tradition – in philosophy, in mysticism, in Oriental religion – which refuses to remain content with this situation, and constantly yearns to break through to a non-duality, to a *coincidence* of opposites, to a higher all-embracing unity . . .

God for Nicholas (of Cusa) is to be seen always 'beyond the coincidence of contradictories . . . and nowhere this side thereof'. In other words, God is not *one* of the poles of traditional theism, but transcends these inevitable finite distinctions. To express this within the logic of non-contradiction is of course finally impossible.

Wilfred Cantwell Smith believes that we must give up asking the question 'Is Christianity true or false?' because it cannot be answered. Instead we should ask the question 'Is *my* Christianity true? Can this belief *become true* to me?' What we must search for is:

. . a new type of answer; neither a simple 'yes' nor a simple 'no' but some *tertium quid*, more subtle, more complex, tentative, yet to be hammered out.

There is so much diversity and clash, so much chaos, in the Christian Church today that the old ideal of a unified or systematic Christian truth has gone. For this, the ecumenical movement is too late. What has happened . . . is that the Christian world has moved into that situation where the Hindu has long been: of open variety, of optional alternatives. It would seem no longer possible for anyone to be told, or even to imagine that he can be told, what it means or should mean, formally and generically, to be a Christian. He must decide for himself – and only for himself.

He even makes the breath-taking assertion that Christians in the past never really claimed that Christianity was *true*.

I have urged the personalist quality of religious life as of ultimate significance, over against the abstract system ... It is a surprisingly modern aberration for anyone to think that Christianity is true or that Islam is – since the Enlightenment, basically, when Europe began to postulate religions as intellectualist systems, patterns of doctrine, so that they could for the first time be labelled 'Christianity' and 'Buddhism', and could be called true or false. Earlier this was not so. No classical Christian theologian, I have discovered, ever said that Christianity is true.

This abandonment of the search for objective truth in religion leads Cantwell Smith to accept the existentialist concept of faith (see p. 61).

This general approach is rapidly becoming established dogma in theology. But there are those who do not fail to realize what is involved, and who realize that this approach means the abandonment of any search for truth in the original sense.

Alasdair MacIntyre:

To introduce a contradiction is to introduce into one's system of thought a licence to say anything.

Lewis Carroll, the author of *Alice in Wonderland*, was a professor of mathematics at Oxford between 1855 and 1881. Although he could not have any idea of what the philosophical and theological debates of the twentieth century would be, he was well aware of what it means for the 'ordinary man' to live in a world in which the laws of logic go by the board. It becomes like the game of Wonderland croquet:

Alice soon came to the conclusion that it was a very difficult game indeed.

The players all played at once without waiting for turns, quarrelling all the while, and fighting for the hedgehogs; and in a very short time the Queen was in a furious passion, and went stamping about, and shouting, 'Off with his head!' or 'Off with her head!' about once in a minute ...

'I don't think they play at all fairly,' Alice began, in a rather complaining tone 'and they all quarrel so dreadfully one can't hear oneself speak – and they don't seem to have any rules in particular; at least, if there are, nobody attends to them ... and I should have croqueted the Queen's hedgehog just now, only it ran away when it saw mine coming!'

Or it is like a world in which words no longer define or describe anything with any accuracy:

Alice ... went on: '– and I thought I'd try and find my way to the top of that hill –'

'When you say "hill",' the Queen interrupted, '*I* could show you hills, in comparison with which you'd call that a valley.'

'No, I shouldn't', said Alice, surprised into contradicting her at last; 'a hill *can't* be a valley, you know. That would be nonsense –'

The Red Queen shook her head. 'You may call it "non-sense" if you like,' she said, 'but *I've*

Writing under the famous pen-name of Lewis Carroll, Dr Charles Dodgson was a nineteenth-century Oxford mathematics lecturer.

heard nonsense, compared with which that would be as sensible as a dictionary!'

Alice curtseyed again, as she was afraid from the Queen's tone of voice that she was a *little* offended; and they walked on in silence till they got to the top of the little hill.

It is also like wandering into the wood where things have no names:

'This must be the wood,' she said thoughtfully to herself, 'where things have no names. I wonder what'll become of *my* name when I go in? I shouldn't like to lose it at all – because they'd have to give me another, and it would almost certainly be an ugly one . . .'
She was rambling on in this way when she reached the wood: it looked very cool and shady. 'Well, at any rate it's a great comfort,' she said as she stepped under the trees, 'after being so hot, to get into the – into the – into *what*?' she went on, rather surprised at not being able to think of the word. 'I mean to get under the – under the – under *this*, you know!' putting her hand on the trunk of the tree. 'What *does* it call itself? I do believe it's got no name – why, to be sure it hasn't!'

She stood silent for a minute, thinking: then she suddenly began again. 'Then it really *has* happened, after all! And now who am I? I *will* remember, if I can! I'm determined to do it!' But being determined didn't help her much, and all she could say, after a great deal of puzzling, was 'L, I *know* it begins with L!'

Doubt extends even to the natural world— with far-reaching effects

Agnosticism begins by doubting whether we can ever know anything for certain about the meaning of the universe or about the truth of Christianity. But sooner or later it leads to doubt as to whether we can know anything for certain even about the physical world which we can see.

Voltaire (1694–1778):

From the stars to the earth's centre, in the external world and within ourselves, every substance is unknown to us. We see appearances only; we are in a dream.

Hannah Arend sums up the agnostic's dilemma in this way:

Descartes' philosophy is haunted by two nightmares which in a sense became the nightmares of the whole modern age, not because this age was so deeply influenced by Cartesian philosophy, but because their emergence was almost inescapable once the true implications of the modern world view were understood. These nightmares are very simple and very well known. In the one, reality, the reality of the world as well as of human life, is doubted; if neither the senses nor common sense nor reason can be trusted, then it may well be that all that we take for reality is only a dream. The other concerns the general human condition as it was revealed by the new discoveries and the impossibility for man to trust his senses and his reason . . .

Colin Wilson says of the atmosphere of Sartre's novel *Nausea*:
In the Journal, we watch the breaking-down of all Roquentin's values. Exhaustion limits him more and more to the present, the here-now. The work of memory, which gives events sequence and coherence, is failing, leaving him more and more dependent for meaning on what he can see and touch. It is Hume's scepticism becoming instinctive, all destroying. All he can see and touch is unrecognizable, unaided by memory; like a photograph of a familiar object taken from an unfamiliar angle. He looks at a seat, and fails to recognize it: 'I murmur: It's a seat, but the word stays on my lips. It refuses to go and put itself on the thing . . . Things are divorced from their names. They are there, grotesque, stubborn, huge, and it seems ridiculous to call them seats, or to say anything at all about them. I am in the midst of things – nameless things.'

Thomas Mann's novels have something of the same atmosphere:

The entire world has become a sort of dialectical nightmare. There are no more certitudes. (Michael Harrington)

This kind of attitude to the natural world can have some very far-reaching consequences in practice.

Bronowski:

The cultures of the East still differ from ours as they did then. They still belittle man as individual man. Under this runs an indifference to the world of the senses, of which the indifference to experienced fact is one face. Anyone who has worked in the East knows how hard it is there to get an answer to a question of fact. When I had to study the casualties from the atomic bombs in Japan at the end of the war, I was dogged and perplexed by this difficulty. The man I asked, whatever man one asks, does not really understand what one wants to know: or rather, he does not understand that one wants to know. He wants to do what is fitting, he is not unwilling to be candid, but at bottom he does not know the facts because they are not his language. These cultures of the East have remained fixed because they lack the language and the very habit of fact.

The fatal flaw in this kind of scepticism, however, is that you cannot consistently *live* with it. *Hume*, for example, was very well aware of the logical conclusion of his scepticism. But these were ideas which he thought about in his study; he realized that he could not actually live as if they were true.

Carelessness and inattention alone can afford us any remedy. For this reason I rely entirely upon them; and take it for granted, whatever may be the reader's opinion at this present moment, that an hour hence he will be persuaded there is both an external and an internal world.

Most fortunately it happens, that since reason is incapable of dispelling these clouds, Nature herself suffices to that purpose, and cures me of this philosophical melancholy and delirium, either by relaxing this bent of mind, or by some avocation and lively impression of my senses, which obliterate all these chimeras. I dine, I play a game of backgammon, I converse, and am merry with my friends; and when, after three or four hours' amusement, I would return to these speculations, they appear so cold, and strained and ridiculous, that I cannot find in my heart to enter into them any further.

Scepticism about others; self-doubt

When agnosticism is linked with psychological determinism, we question every motivation in ourselves and in others, to such an extent that we cannot be sure about the 'real self' any longer.

Maurice Friedman quotes some words of Martin Buber about these consequences:

This unmasking begins in the service of truth . . . Yet it ends, paradoxically, by making all truth questionable and by undermining the foundations of existence between men. 'One no longer fears that the other will voluntarily dissemble', writes Martin Buber in a statement on 'existential mistrust'. One simply takes it for granted that he cannot do otherwise.

'I do not really take cognizance of his communication as knowledge . . . Rather I listen for what drives the other to say what he says, for an unconscious motive, say, or a "complex" . . . My main task in my intercourse with my fellow-man becomes more and more, whether in terms of individual psychology or sociology, to see through and unmask him. In the classical case this in no wise means a mask he has put on to deceive me, but a mask that has, without his knowing it, been put on him, indeed positively imprinted on him, so that what is really deceived is his own consciousness.'

C. E. M. Joad writes about the very practical effect of this approach:

The belief that men's views reflect their desires rather than their reason, has a number of harmful effects in practice. For example, it is destructive of good talk and inimical to fruitful discussion. Owing to the influence of psycho-analysis there prevails in modern society a refusal to discuss any view on its merits. If X expresses an opinion Y, the question discussed is not whether Y is true or at least reasonable, but the considerations which led X to believe it to be true. Objective truth being regarded as unobtainable, what alone is thought interesting are the reasons which led people to formulate their particular brand of error.

Bunuel's film *Belle de Jour* portrays both the real world and a world of fantasy at the same time, in such a way that one can never be sure what is going on.

Most audiences will not find anything visually shocking about *Belle de Jour*. They will find instead a cumulative mystery: What is really happening and what is not? . . . The film continues – switching back and forth between Severine's real and fantasy worlds so smoothly that after a while it becomes impossible to say which is which . . . There is no way of knowing – and this seems to be the point of the film with which Bunuel says he is winding up his 40-year career. Fantasy, he seems to be saying, is nothing but the human dimension of reality that makes life tolerable, and sometimes even fun.

Harold Pinter in his plays portrays this kind of world in which certainties about people have dissolved:

The desire for verification is understandable, but cannot always be satisfied. There are no hard distinctions between what is real and what is unreal, nor between what is true and what is false. The thing is not necessarily either true or false; it can be both true and false. The assumption that to verify what has happened and what is happening presents few problems, I take to be inaccurate. A character on the stage who can present no convincing argument or information as to his past experiences, his present behaviour or his aspirations, nor give a comprehensive analysis of his motives is as legitimate and as worthy of attention as one who, alarmingly, can do all these things. The more acute the experience the less articulate its expression.

 ## Loss of content and direction in the arts

If we cannot be sure that we know anything about ourselves or others or about the external world, this is bound to affect the content of what the artist is communicating. The content is going to become thinner and thinner.

Eric Rhode:

During the past decade a revolution has taken place in the arts, and nowhere more decisively than in the cinema. You could describe it crudely by saying that the distinction between high and lowbrow culture has been abandoned. Someone making movies now doesn't have to limit himself to serious subjects in order to be taken seriously. He isn't expected to explore the implications of his theme, or to have an emotional or intellectual commitment to it. The reign of Mindlessness has begun. Susan Sontag says that she's 'against interpretation', against content. Our attention, she believes, should be mainly directed to questions of form and technique.

This notion appears to be widely accepted, and examples of it can be found almost everywhere. In a letter recently published in the *Listener*, Allan King praises Robert Flaherty's *Louisiana Story*'because it has 'no intellectual or verbal information content to speak of': an assumption that would have shocked Flaherty.

Simon Hoggart, writing about a Conference on Broadcasting:

The greater danger is, and this was amply illustrated by the conference, that we are reaching a stage in which television is only assessed in terms of either ratings or 'suitability to the medium'. The latter is a dropping from McLuhan; if the medium is the message, then the message becomes irrelevant, and we can only discuss quality in terms of how well a production fits the arrangement of light pulses we see on our screens. Baverstock was reduced to calling excellence 'the best talent with the best technical facilities', a statement which tells us nothing at all.

 ## Science modifies its claim to discover 'truth'

In the early period of modern science, it was confidently believed that the scientist was engaged in the pursuit of 'the truth' about the universe. By observation and experiment, he believed that he would eventually be able to formulate reliable theories about how the universe works. Scientists today, however, make a very much more limited claim about what they are doing:

Bronowski:

It is not possible for the brain to arrive at *certain* knowledge. All those formal systems, in mathematics and physics and the philosophy of science, which claim to give foundations for certain truth are surely mistaken. I am tempted to say that we do not look for truth, but for knowledge. But I dislike this form of words, for two reasons. First of all, we do *look* for truth, however we define it; it is what we *find* that is knowledge. And second, what we fail to find is not truth but certainty; the nature of truth is exactly the knowledge that we do find ... No knowledge can be certain that continues to expand with us as we live inside the growing flesh of our experience.

Wren-Lewis:

The modern theories are never more than models to suggest new lines of practical action, and therefore capable of being discarded at any time in favour of radically new models in a way which would be impossible if they were attempts to express the hidden truth behind phenomena. Experimental science succeeds by finding truth in experience, in action, and this is utterly incompatible with the traditional outlook on the world both logically and psychologically.

The following extract is from a review by Douglas Spanner of the book *The Survival of God in the Scientific Age* by Alan Isaacs:

Dr. Isaac's humanism has no place for Truth ... Science has often been regarded as 'the disinterested search for Truth'. To express it thus is simply to imply that in some sense truth is an absolute, already existent and awaiting the searcher; but this is too near to being a concession to the theologians to be acceptable to the rationalist. Science has been held to seek truth in two respects at least; with regard to its *facts*, and with regard to its *theories*.

However, as Dr. Isaacs rightly points out, 'the scientist no longer talks about facts as if there were fragments of the truth. The word "fact", the scientist now sees, involves highly emotional ideas which are of much greater use to lawyers and theologians.' Instead, 'science deals not with facts but with observations.' The difference? Simply facts are things conceived of as true in themselves, *i.e. absolutely*; observations, on the other hand, are *relative* to the observer, and the relationship conditions their validity. Thus we slip our moorings!

Dr. Isaacs reveals by the whole tenor of his argument, that truth is no longer his goal; what he seeks for is rather *validity for the moment*.

This is how *C. S. Lewis* interpreted some of these developments in modern science:

Men became scientific because they expected Law in nature, and they expected Law in nature because they believed in a Legislator. In most modern scientists this belief has died: it will be interesting to see how their confidence in uniformity survives it. Two significant developments have already appeared – the hypothesis of a lawless subnature, and the surrender of the claim that science is true. We may be living nearer than we suppose to the end of the Scientific Age.

Professional philosophy abandons its search for truth

Traditional philosophy has always been concerned with the pursuit of the truth. Now, however, philosophers generally have abandoned the search for truth in the older sense, and have been forced to limit the field of their enquiries to, for example, the study of concepts, and the study of the meaning of words.

G. J. Warnock in *English Philosophy since 1900* writes:

The proper concern of philosophy is with concepts, with the ways and means by which we think and communicate.

Ernest Gellner writes with scorn and despair over this betrayal of philosophy. This is how his attitude is summed up by Leslie Paul:

This has given rise to a paradox worthy of *Beyond the Fringe* that not a few philosophers disbelieve in philosophy: they believe that philosophy is the pathology of language and their own role, as diagnosticians and therapists of linguistic mistakes, is to catch out the chaps who indulge in it. It is as if, the sociologist Ernest Gellner said, ... swimming instructors no longer believed it possible to swim. In an epigram not easily forgotten he wrote, 'A cleric who loses his faith abandons his calling, a philosopher who loses his, redefines his subject.'

'The view that the needle *must* be in the haystack is extremely powerful, and operative in making philosophers seek it. The needle has not turned up. But the burrowing in this haystack has become habitual and established, and a cessation of it would leave men in a bewildered state. Some have no other skills. So, some alternative positions have emerged and are to be found: there *may* be needles in the haystack. Haystacks are interesting. We like hay.'

 ## 'Truth-substitutes' fill the vacuum

People would *like* to know the truth, and life seems to work better when we know something of the true facts of our condition. But what if we reach the position when we feel that we cannot hope to know the truth about ourselves and the universe?

One answer is to say that what really matters is not so much the *truth* of what we believe, but the *sincerity* with which we believe it.

George Eliot:

I have too profound a conviction of the efficacy that lies in all sincere faith, and the spiritual blight that comes with no faith, to have any negative propagandism in me ... I care only to know, if possible, the lasting meaning that lies in all religious doctrine from the beginning till now.

Another answer is to say that we should simply live *as if* what we believe is true. We cannot be sure that it is 'the truth'; and we must therefore simply live on the assumption that it *is* true.

Lessing's Parable of the Three Rings:

There was once an ancient ring which had the power to bestow upon its owner the gift of being loved by God and man. This was passed on down many generations until it came into the possession of a father who had three sons equally dear to him. To resolve the dilemma, he had two replicas made and gave a ring to each son. After his death all three claimed to possess the true ring. But as with religion, the original cannot be traced. Historical investigation is of no avail. But a wise judge counsels each son to behave as if he had the true ring and prove it by deeds of love. Thus in the end it will not matter who had the original.

Another possible answer is to say that we should stop asking the question 'is it *true*?' and ask instead 'does it *work*?'

William James:

If the hypothesis of God works satisfactorily in the widest sense of the word, it is true.

Thomas Arnold:

All societies of men, whether we call them states or churches, should make their bond to consist in a common object and a common practice rather than in a common belief; in other words, their end should be good rather than truth.

J. B. Priestley:

We can try to feel and think and behave, to some extent, *as if* our society were already beginning to be contained by religion, as if we were certain that Man cannot even remain Man unless he looks beyond himself, as if we were finding our way home again in the universe.

Up to this point we have been thinking in terms of private and personal beliefs of individuals. If we cannot hope to find the truth, then we must leave each individual to reconcile himself to the situation as best as he can. But what if some individual or some group comes into a position of power and then proceeds to *tell* the people what the truth is, and what is good and right? This is precisely what has happened in Communism.

André Gide:

In Marxist doctrine there is no such thing as truth – at least not in the absolute sense – there is only relative truth.

George Orwell in *1984*:

Doublethink means the power of holding two contradictory beliefs simultaneously, and accepting both of them. The party intellectual knows that he is playing tricks with reality, but by the exercise of doublethink he also satisfies himself that reality is not violated.

Arthur Koestler, writing about 'the comforts of double-think':

Behind the curtain there is the magic world of double-think. 'Ugly is beautiful, false is true, and also conversely.' This is not Orwell; it was written in all seriousness by the late Professor Suzuki, the foremost propounder of modern Zen, to illustrate the principle of the identity of opposites ... Facts and arguments which succeed in penetrating the outer defences are processed by the dialectical method until 'false' becomes 'true', tyranny the true democracy, and a herring a racehorse.

This approach to truth in Communism has some very practical consequences. It means, for example, that the authorities feel perfectly free to tell any lies they want if it serves their purpose. *Ignazio Silone*, who was for many years a member of the Italian Communist Party, describes an incident which took place at a meeting of the International in Moscow:

They were discussing one day, in a special commission of the Executive, the ultimatum issued by the central committee of the British trade unions, ordering its local branches not to support the Communist-led minority movement, on pain of expulsion. After the representative of the British Communist Party had explained the serious disadvantages of both solutions, because one meant the liquidation of the minority movement and the other the exit of the minority from the trade unions, the Russian delegate Piatnisky put forward a suggestion which seemed as obvious to him as Columbus' egg: 'The branches,' he suggested, 'should declare that they submit to the discipline demanded, and then, in practice, should do exactly the contrary.' The English Communist interrupted: 'But that would be a lie.' Loud laughter greeted this ingenuous objection, frank, cordial, interminable laughter, the like of which the gloomy offices of the Communist International had perhaps never heard before. The joke quickly spread all over Moscow, for the Englishman's entertaining and incredible reply was telephoned at once to Stalin and to the most important offices of State, provoking new waves of mirth everywhere.

Nikita Struve, writing about contemporary Russia and its attitude to Christianity:

What impresses me … is that atheism today seems to have given up the search for truth. Facts and arguments which tell against it are dismissed in silence.

This answer to the question of truth, therefore, opens up the frightening possibility that the horrors of Alice's dream world can be enacted in history.

At this moment the King, who had been for some time busily writing in his notebook, called out, 'Silence!' and read out from his book, 'Rule Forty-two' *All persons more than a mile high to leave the court.*'

Everybody looked at Alice.

'I'm not a mile high,' said Alice.

'You are,' said the King.

'Nearly two miles high,' added the Queen.

'Well, I shan't go, at any rate,' said Alice: 'besides, that's not a regular rule; you invented it just now.'

'It's the oldest rule in the book,' said the King.

'Then it ought to be Number One,' said Alice.

The King turned pale, and shut his notebook hastily. 'Consider your verdict,' he said to the jury in a low trembling voice. . .

. . . said the Queen. 'Sentence first – verdict afterwards.'

John Lehmann, writing about the relevance of *Alice* in today's world:

This procedure, I suggest, though meant as a joke, was uncannily prophetic, and has become too painfully actual in our own age to be treated entirely as a joke.

 ## Truth is sought through some 'experience'

Many who have reached the position of agnosticism have taken to drugs, for example, not simply for excitement and release, but in the hope of being able to find out through this experience what the universe is all about.

Aldous Huxley, in his earlier writings (*e.g. Do What You Will*, 1936), expresses his profound scepticism about the possibility of finding the truth about the universe. (See p. 23.)

In his book *The Doors of Perception* (1954), he advocates the use of drugs such as mescalin:

What happens to the majority of the few who have taken mescalin under supervision can be summarized as follows:

1. The ability to remember and to 'think straight' is little if at all reduced. . .

2. Visual impressions are greatly intensified and the eye recovers some of the perceptual innocence of childhood, when the sensum was not immediately and automatically subordinated to the concept. . .

3. Though the intellect remains unimpaired and though perception is enormously improved, the will suffers a profound change for the worse. The mescalin taker sees no reason for doing anything in particular and finds most of the causes for which, at ordinary times, he was prepared to act and suffer, profoundly uninteresting. He can't be bothered with them, for the good reason that he has better things to think about.

4. These better things may be experienced (as I experienced them) 'out there', or 'in here', or in both worlds, the inner and the outer, simultaneously or successively. That they *are* better seems to be self-evident to all mescalin takers who come to the drug with a sound liver and an untroubled mind. . . .

Other persons discover a world of visionary beauty. To others again is revealed the glory, the infinite value and meaningfulness of naked existence, of the given, unconceptualized event. In the final stage of ego-lessness there is an 'obscure knowledge' that All is in all – that All is actually each. This is as near, I take it, as a finite mind can ever come to 'perceiving everything that is happening everywhere in the universe' . . .

From this . . . excursion into the realm of theory we may now return to the miraculous facts – four bamboo chair legs in the middle of a room. Like Wordsworth's daffodils, they brought all manner of wealth – the gift beyond price, of a new direct insight into the very Nature of Things, together with a more modest treasure of understanding in the field, especially, of the arts.

Towards the end of his life he was still advocating the use of drugs as a way of 'knowing'.

A scene from the BBC Television production of George Orwell's play 1984, *a prophetic drama about life in a totalitarian state.*

5. THE ANSWER OF CHRISTIAN EXISTENTIALISM

"We can know Christianity is true only by a leap of faith"

The answer of most modern theologians has been that Christian claims to the truth are at best improbable, and at worst absurd; they are an offence to the intellect. Christian beliefs are not so much beyond the understanding (as in Answer 2); they are against the understanding. Reason and feeling are not able to find the truth; rationalism leads to a dead end. Faith and scientific knowledge have little or nothing in common; they belong to two different worlds. If we are to find the truth, therefore, we will find it only by committing ourselves to the truth in a 'leap of faith'. We cannot hope to think out the truth and analyse it rationally. We can only experience it in all its absurdity and contradiction.

This answer was formulated by Soren Kierkegaard (see p. 64) and was first introduced into theology by Karl Barth (p. 66). The following quotations are from theologians who have accepted, to a greater or lesser extent, Kierkegaard's understanding of faith. It may well be objected that it is grossly unfair and misleading to group these writers together in one category. Barth and Brunner, for example, have very different attitudes to natural theology, and have been openly and fiercely critical of each other's writing. Some of these writers would call the resurrection a 'myth', while others would insist that it was a historical event. The crucial point at issue here, however, is the answer to the question 'How can I know if Christianity is true?' And however much these writers may differ from one another in certain areas of theology, they all share a common starting-point because they give very similar answers to the basic question.

SOME TWENTIETH-CENTURY VIEWS

Emil Brunner:

When a believer is asked: Why do you believe that Jesus is the Christ? he can only answer: Why should I not believe, since Jesus confronts me as the Christ, when He meets me in the story and the witness of the Apostles as the Christ? It is not the believer who needs to give reasons, but the unbeliever ... It is not the one who accepts this claim of Jesus, and obeys it, who has to give 'reasons' for his faith; on the contrary, those who do not accept this claim ought to state the 'reasons' for their decision ... These reasons ... do not belong to the sphere of academic knowledge, but to the sphere of one's philosophy of life, of self-knowledge, of faith.

Paul Tillich:

Sometimes ... a wave of light breaks into our darkness, and it is as though a voice were saying: 'You are accepted. *You are accepted*, accepted by that which is greater than you, and the name of which you do not know. Do not ask for the name now; perhaps you will find it later. Do not try to do anything now; perhaps you will do much. Do not seek for anything; do not perform anything; do not intend anything. *Simply accept the fact that you are accepted.*'

Absolute faith is 'the accepting of the acceptance without somebody or something that accepts'.

Rudolph Bultmann:

Christ meets us in the preaching as one crucified and risen. He meets us in the word of preaching and nowhere else. The faith of Easter is just this—the faith in the word of preaching. It would be wrong for us at this point to raise again the problem of how this preaching arose historically, as though that could vindicate its truth. That would be to tie our faith in the word of God to the results of historical research. The word of preaching confronts us as the Word of God. It is not for us to question its credentials. It is we who are questioned, we who are asked whether we will believe the word or reject it.

It is precisely its immunity from proof which secures the Christian proclamation against the charge of being mythological.

The real purpose of myth is not to present an objective picture of the world as it is, but to express man's understanding of himself in the world in which he lives. Myth should be interpreted not cosmologically, but anthropologically, or better still, existentially.

Wilfred Cantwell Smith:

To say that Christianity is true is to say nothing significant; the only question that concerns either God, or me, or my neighbour is whether *my* Christianity is true, and whether yours is. And to that question, a truly cosmic one, in my case the only valid answer is a sorrowful 'not very'. By my Christianity I mean my actual, living Christianity, my Christianness, the specific religion of my personal life...

Furthermore, my Christianity may be more true this morning than it was yesterday afternoon. It may collapse altogether in some crisis tomorrow morning ... Again, one man's Christianity may be (must be) more false than another's. Your Christianity may be truer than the Christianity of your next-door neighbour.

Teilhard de Chardin believes that evolution faces us with a choice between absolute optimism and absolute pessimism. Our choice between them amounts to a leap of faith, because there is no tangible evidence which points one way or the other.

What makes the world in which we live specifically modern is our discovery in it and around it of evolution. And I can now add that what disconcerts the modern world at its very roots is not being sure, and not seeing how it ever could be sure, that there is an outcome – *a suitable outcome* – to that evolution.

Either nature is closed to our demands for futurity, in which case thought, the fruit of millions of years of effort, is stifled, stillborn in a self-abortive and absurd universe. Or else an opening exists—that of the super-soul above our souls; but in that case the way out, if we are to agree to embark on it, must open out freely on to limitless psychic spaces in a universe to which we can unhesitatingly entrust ourselves.

Between these two alternatives of absolute optimism or absolute pessimism, there is no middle way because by its very nature progress is all or nothing. We are confronted accordingly with two directions and two only: one upwards and the other downwards, and there is no possibility of finding a half-way house.

On neither side is there any tangible evidence to produce. Only, in support of hope, there are rational invitations to an act of faith.

John Robinson holds that to say that 'God is love' is an act of faith in the face of all the evidence:

For this way of thinking, to say that 'God is personal' is to say that 'reality at its very deepest level is personal', that personality is of *ultimate* significance in the constitution of the universe, that in personal relationships we touch the final meaning of existence as nowhere else ... To believe in God as love means to believe that in pure personal relationship we encounter, not merely what ought to be, but what is, the deepest, veriest truth about the structure of reality. This, in face of all the evidence, is a tremendous act of faith. But it is not the feat of persuading oneself of the existence of a super-Being beyond this world endowed with personal qualities. Belief in God is the trust, the well-nigh incredible trust, that to give ourselves to the uttermost in love is not to be confounded but to be 'accepted', that Love is the ground of our being, to which ultimately we 'come home'.

Statements of faith, to his mind, cannot be proved or disproved:

To affirm belief in God is indeed to assert a faith in how things are . . . It is to say that we can trust the universe not only at the level of certain mathematical regularities but at the level of utterly personal reliability that Jesus indicated by the word 'Abba, Father!' It is the faith that this is as true and objective a picture of reality as that described by the natural sciences, and more fundamental . . .

God-statements are statements about the veracity of this relationship. They cannot be proved or disproved, any more than human trust or love can finally be proved or disproved. In that sense there is nothing that might occur, as Anthony Flew has demanded there should be, which would show conclusively that there is no God.

Alan Richardson is basically committed to Kierkegaard's leap of faith:

Subjectivity becomes the key to certitude when we take what Kierkegaard called 'the leap of faith', when we learn to trust, to obey and worship. Thus belief or faith in the true biblical and religious sense is not temporary acceptance of an hypothesis until proof or disproof is forthcoming. Belief in God is altogether misrepresented by being given the status of an explanatory hypothesis . . . Faith in God is essentially a relationship between persons, and therefore is no more susceptible of scientific proof or disproof than is a woman's trusting, obedient and respecting love for her husband . . . The escape from subjectivity in the sense of self-imprisonment is therefore not by argument but by commitment, obedience and worship . . . The 'verification principle' of existential truth is commitment to it in faith, obedience and worship . . . In the last analysis the verification principle of existential truth is a subjective one.

But he adds certain important qualifications:

We do not suppose that there are ultimately two kinds of knowledge or two kinds of truth. In the final analysis truth is one and every particular truth coheres with all other truth . . . Truth is a unity . . . Thus when we speak of two kinds of knowledge we must not be understood to imply that there is any fundamental contradiction between scientific and other ways of knowing.

This does not mean that there is no place for rational intellect and scientific investigation in the sphere of religious truth . . . There are criteria of Christian truths (namely, truths of history as recited in the creed) which acquit Christianity from being 'merely' subjective.

Rosemary Haughton wants to draw the attention of the questioner away from questions about presuppositions to consider the character of Jesus himself. It is assumed that what Jesus was and did will be self-authenticating and commend itself as true, quite independently of other assumptions about God and man.

We do not know and cannot know in any ordinary sense what is the reality to which we refer by the great symbolic opening phrases of the creed. If all the rest depended on answering the question 'What is God?' we would not get much further. But what we often fail to notice is the fact that these very phrases do not refer to a being as such but rather to a series of relationships. It is in the relationships that we discover the reality, whatever it may be. Christ himself never answered the question, 'What is God?' When Philip asked him, 'Lord, show us the Father', the answer he got was, 'He who has seen me has seen the Father'.

Leslie Paul:

It cannot be said that what emerges from my survey is a 'proved' Christianity and a 'disproved' humanism, or vice versa. This has not been the object of the exercise. In any case, one is not moving in the realm of proof or disproof, adding up lists of pros and cons for this view or that and striking a credit balance here and a debit there, but in a dimension of reflection and contemplation upon public and private experience which thrusts us deeper and deeper into the human dilemma. It is a spiritual enterprise bound to be anguished as we grope for meanings given to the heart and the poetic intuition as much as to the head.

The New Dutch Catechism, while it insists on a real historical resurrection interprets the first eleven chapters of Genesis as 'myth' in the sense that Bultmann uses the word (see p. 61). 'These chapters have nothing to do with history, and our acceptance of the Christian assumptions they teach therefore becomes a leap of faith. We accept this outlook not because we have good reason to believe that it is true, but because it appeals to us.'

The first eleven chapters of Genesis tell of the origins of mankind – Adam, Cain, Noah and Babel. We know that they are not descriptions of disconnected historical facts. They go deeper. The narratives are symbols in which the kernel of all human history is described, including that which is still to come. Adam is man. Cain is to be found in the newspapers and may be seen within our own heart. Noah and the builders of Babel – they are ourselves. Chapters 1–11 of Genesis describe the basic elements of all human encounter with God. It is only with Chapter 12, where Abraham appears, that we begin to make out historical figures in the past.

We have seen what the story of paradise and the fall intended to convey: the purpose of God, as realized in the whole, and above all in the end. We really know nothing of the actual beginnings.

THREE KEY FIGURES

Blaise Pascal (1623–1662)

Pascal shows traces of this kind of answer in his approach.

▷ He makes a distinction between 'the heart' and 'the reason':

The heart has its reasons which are unknown to reason . . . It is the heart which is aware of God and not reason. This is what faith is: God perceived intuitively by the heart, not by reason.

In making this distinction, he is continuing the dichotomy which we have noticed in Aquinas, Locke and others:

The heart = 'the intuitive spirit'

The Reason, Mind = 'the geometric spirit'

What he did was to erect a dualism of his own in which two realms existed: one of the heart and one of the mind. In religion, unlike Descartes, he applied the logic of the heart. In mathematics and physics, however, Pascal used the same geometry as did Descartes. (Bronowski and Mazlish)

Blaise Pascal, French mathematician and philosopher.

Soren Kierkegaard was born in Copenhagen, where he studied at the University before going on to Berlin.

▷ He puts forward the idea of 'The Wager': Christianity cannot be proved conclusively by the reason, but neither can it be disproved. If it turns out that Christianity is true, we have everything to gain; but if it turns out to be false, we have nothing to lose. We should accept the inevitable risk of faith, and gamble on the truth of Christianity.

This was the essential step of Pascal: that doubt leads to faith, because doubt makes it certain that there is no answer to the question of self-consciousness. The view of Pascal was that the answer to the epistemological question is – that there is no rational answer. We must simply place our bet on faith. (Bronowski and Mazlish)

Soren Kierkegaard (1813–1855)

Pascal was very much of an isolated philosopher and had no following. Kierkegaard, similarly, was very much of an individualist in his philosophy, and had no following during his lifetime. But during this century he has suddenly become popular, and has become the source not only of Secular Existentialism, but also of Christian Existentialism.

He built his position on the position reached by Hume and Kant; *i.e.* he accepted the impossibility of finding certain knowledge through the senses. And he accepted Kant's distinction between *noumena* and *phenomena*. He is very conscious, however, that he is breaking completely new ground:

My task is so new that there is literally no one in the 1800 years of Christianity from whom I can learn how I should proceed.

His position and the direction his views have taken can be summed up as follows:

▷ There is no point in asking 'What is "the truth"?' because it is impossible to know the truth objectively. The question we must ask is 'What is the truth *for me*? How am *I* to live my life?'

The thing is to understand myself, to see what God really wishes *me* to do; the thing is to find a truth which is true *for me*, to find *the idea for which I can live and die*.

▷ Reasoning will lead us only to paradox; and historical enquiry leads only to probability, which is without value for faith.

If from such a point of view we enquire about the truth objectively, then we see that truth is a *paradox*.

If the contemporary generation had left nothing behind them but these words: 'We believed that in such and such a year God appeared among us in our community, and finally died,' it would be more than enough. The contemporary generation would have done all that was necessary: for this little advertisement, this *nota bene* on a page of universal history, would be sufficient to afford an occasion for a successor, and the most voluminous account can in all eternity do nothing more.

On the title page of *Philosophical Fragments or a Fragment of Philosophy* he puts the question:

Is an historical point of departure possible for an eternal consciousness; how can such a point of departure have any other than a merely historical interest; is it possible to base an eternal happiness upon historical knowledge?

▷ Christian beliefs are absurd; they are an offence to the reason. Christian faith, therefore, means believing *against* the reason, *against* the understanding.

... the paradox (of the Christian faith) cannot and shall not be understood ... the task is to hold fast to this and to endure the crucifixion of the understanding.

A believer who believes, *i.e.* believes against the understanding, takes the mystery of faith seriously and is not duped by the pretence of understanding.

Here is such a definition of truth: *objective incertitude, clung to and appropriated with passionate inwardness, is truth*, the highest truth that there can be, *for one who exists*.

The emphasis in faith is on the *will* rather than on the intellect:

Christianity, . . . or becoming a Christian, has nothing to do with a change in the intellect - but in the will. But this change is the most painful of all operations, comparable to vivisection . . . And because it is so terrible, becoming

a Christian in Christendom has long since . . . been transformed into a change of the intellect.

Faith therefore depends entirely on the choice of the will. It is a huge risk.

And so I say to myself: I choose; that historical fact means so much to me that I decide to stake my whole life upon it. Then he lives; lives entirely full of the idea of risking his life for it: and his life is the proof that he believes. He did not have a few proofs, and so believed and then began to live. No, the very reverse.

That is called risking; and without risk faith is an impossibility. *To be related to spirit means to undergo a test;* to believe, to wish to believe, is to change one's life into a trial; daily test is the trial of faith.

Faith must be existential faith.

From the Christian point of view faith belongs to the existential; God did not appear in the character of a professor who has some doctrines which must first be believed and then understood.

No, faith belongs to and has its home in the existential, and in all eternity it has nothing to do with knowledge as a comparative or a superlative.

Faith expresses a relation from personality to personality.

Personality is not a sum of doctrines, nor is it something directly accessible ... Personality is that which is within ... it is that which is within to which a man, himself in turn a personality, may be related in faith. Between person and person no other relation is possible. Take the two most passionate lovers who have ever lived, and even if they are, as is said, one soul in two bodies, this can never come to anything more than that the one believes that the other loves him or her.

In this purely personal relation between God as personal being and the believer as personal being, in *existence*, is to be found the concept of faith.

(Hence the apostolic formula, 'the obedience of faith' (*e.g.* Romans 1:5), so that faith tends to the will and personality, not to intellectuality – *marginal note*.)

This is how two writers who are not Christians (Herbert Read and H. J. Blackham) sum up Kierkegaard's position regarding the nature of Christian faith:

'Faith expresses a relation from personality to personality ... In this purely personal relation between God as personal being and the believer as personal being, in *existence*, is to be found the concept of faith.' The whole of Kierkegaard's philosophy revolves round this axiom . . .

What one realizes, in reading these late extracts from the *Journals*, is the absolute intransigence of the egoism which Kierkegaard made the basis of his faith.

In rejecting Christianity, Kierkegaard had perceived the discontinuity between faith and reason, and in rejecting speculative philosophy he retained this perception and built his position upon it. He made it the effort of his life to renew the meaning of Christianity by compelling recognition of the permanent cleavage between faith and reason . . .

Kierkegaard's argument deals with the object of Christian faith and the manner of apprehending it.

That a man born and living in history says that he is God and dies in humiliation plunges into a dilemma those who would build their lives on him and his word. Nothing has happened since to enlighten by one scruple the strain on belief. The historical success of Christianity is worthless evidence. The present generation is exactly in the position of the contemporaries of Christ who witnessed his humiliation on the cross. Faith today, unless it is faith in the faith of the Apostles, is not other than their faith in the man who makes the most absurd of claims. The truth of this claim cannot in the nature of the case be made objectively certain, or even investigated; on the contrary the absolute discontinuity between the human and the divine which inheres in the conception of God makes it unthinkable, so that it cannot by any human mind be recognized as true, cannot be entertained as a possibility . . . If a man claims to be God, then all that reason can do is to take notice of this claim and give special attention to all the circumstances attending to it. Inquiry into the authenticity of the evidence (itself never finally conclusive) is beside the point, however, for if the historical facts were established beyond cavil the enquirer would be no nearer to making up his mind what to make of them. The incarnation is a paradox which can never be thought nor accepted by reason, and therefore the claim that it is the supreme truth imposes a limit on thought and throws the enquirer into a passion of uncertainty. If, by the grace of God he sets reason and experience aside and joins himself to the paradox in the passion of faith, he is 'out upon the deep, over 70,000 fathoms of water' and risks everything. The decision to take the risk cannot bring certainty. The intelligibility of the paradox remains absolute, incapable of being reduced or got round. Its acceptance by faith does nothing to reduce its offence to reason; it is a perpetual tension with the intelligence, a cause of suffering and passion, reducing the most powerful understanding to the level of the most simple, and both to nothing; for it poses itself as the limit of all thought, and the question at issue is eternal happiness.

Karl Barth (1886–1968)

It was Karl Barth who first introduced Kierkegaard's ideas into theology, and he has been a major – if not *the* major – influence in theology in the first half of the twentieth century. We shall therefore examine his thinking in some detail. The quotations summarizing his position are from T. F. Torrance, *Karl Barth: An Introduction to his Early Theology, 1910–1931.*

His debt to liberalism. Barth grew up within the tradition of the liberal theology of the nineteenth century, and he admits that he was at one stage a liberal theologian. However, in August 1914 he was appalled to find that many of his theological teachers had joined other German intellectuals in a manifesto supporting Kaiser Wilhelm II's war policy.

Disillusioned by their conduct, I perceived that I should not be able any longer to accept their ethics and dogmatics, their biblical exegesis, their interpretation of history, that at least for me the theology of the nineteenth century had no future.

There were two fatal weaknesses which he detected in nineteenth-century theology:

▷ It accommodated Christianity to the assumptions of the nineteenth century which were basically the assumptions inherited from the Enlightenment.

▷ This meant in practice that theology suffered from a cancerous subjectivism; Schleiermacher could only speak of God by speaking of man in a loud voice. Thus since God was so reduced, Christianity tended towards mere humanism or pantheism.

In spite of this, however, Barth continued to accept many of the methods and conclusions of liberal scholars about the Bible.

His debt to Kierkegaard. In setting out to

Dr Karl Barth, Theologian and Professor at Basle University.

make a new beginning, he drew certain important ideas from Kierkegaard:

▷ He thought of God as 'Wholly Other', in reaction against the liberal tendency to make God so like man that he is hardly distinguishable from him. He maintained that there is an 'infinite qualitative difference between God and man':

The Gospel falls upon man as God's own mighty Word, questioning him down to the bottom of his being, uprooting him from his securities and satisfactions, and therefore tearing clean asunder all the relations that keep him prisoner within his own ideals in order that he may be genuinely free for God and for his wonderful new work of grace in Jesus Christ. The emphasis was quite definitely upon what became known as *diastasis*, the distance, the separation, between God's ways and man's ways, God's thoughts and man's thoughts, between Christianity and culture, between Gospel and humanism, between Word of God and word of man.

▷ The concept of 'indirect communication' between God and man:

In Jesus the communication of God begins with a rebuff, with the exposure of a vast chasm, with the clear revelation of a great stumbling-block. Remove from the Christian Religion, as Christendom has done, its ability to shock, and Christianity, by becoming a direct communication, is altogether destroyed. It then becomes a tiny, superficial thing, capable of neither inflicting deep wounds nor of healing them; by discovering an unreal and merely human compassion, it forgets the qualitative distinction between God and man. (Kierkegaard)

Barth acknowledged his debt to Kierkegaard's existentialism and his responsibility for introducing it into theology:

For its introduction into theology, I myself must bear a good deal of unwitting responsibility, for I paid tribute to it in my commentary on the Epistle to the Romans (1921) and even in my well-known false start, the *Christliche Dogmatik in Entwurf* (1927). In the light of these works, and in respect of certain features of my theological thinking in its later development, I must admit that I have learned something from what Kierkegaard and his modern followers teach.

In later years, particularly from 1931 onwards, Barth changed his position considerably. He confessed that he might have been somewhat extreme in the way he had stated his case in his early years. But Kierkegaard's influence had already determined many of his fundamental assumptions. Much of this influence Barth sought later to tone down .and sometimes to cut out altogether.

It is certainly true, therefore, to say that the later Barth is different from the earlier Barth. But on this particular question about the truth of Christianity he has not fundamentally altered his position, and his earlier writings were very influential in the development of modern theology.

His concept of the Word of God. He emphasizes that the Word of God is utterly rational. But at the same time it can not be identified or equated with any particular form of words, even the words of the Bible. Its rationality is so unique that it cannot be related to any kind of rationality as *we* know it.

In Revelation God gives himself to us as the object of our faith and knowledge, but because he remains God the Lord, he does not give himself into our hands, as it were; he does not resign himself to our mastery or our control as if he were a dead object. He remains the living Lord, unqualified in his freedom, whom we can only know in accordance with his acts upon us, by following his movement of grace, and by renouncing on our part any attempt to master him by adapting him to our own schemes of thought or structures of existence; that is, whom we can know only by knowing him out of himself as an objective reality (*Gegenstand*) standing over against us, as the divine Partner and Lord of our knowing of him. A favourite term that Barth uses to describe this unique object of knowledge, which we cannot bring under our own control, is *mystery*. By 'mystery' Barth does not refer to anything a-logical or irrational, but on the contrary to full, complete and self-sufficient rationality, the rationality of God, who is so fully rational that he does not need to be interpreted in terms of anything outside of himself. That is the supreme rationality that confronts us when God gives himself to us to be known as a reality whose possibility resides absolutely

within himself, and whom we cannot understand, far less derive or substantiate, except out of himself. He reveals himself to us in such a way that we can know him only if our thinking begins with his revelation, and follows it through, if it is grounded entirely upon it, and never subjected to any other truth or criterion outside of it.

Even Jesus himself, therefore, is not an unambiguous revelation of God:

In Jesus, God becomes veritably a secret: He is made known as the Unknown, speaking in eternal silence . . .

The Bible is not a means of direct communication between God and man; all it can do is to point beyond itself and bear witness to the Word of God.

The Word of God comes to us in the Bible through the speech of sinful, fallible men to whom God has spoken and who bear witness to his speaking. We do not have here a direct speaking of God from heaven, but a speaking through a transient and imperfect human medium. No doubt the human word we hear in the Scriptures is not always appropriate or adequate to the Word of God which its authors have heard and to which they bear testimony, but nevertheless it is the human word which God has freely chosen and decided to use as the form in which he speaks his Word to us.

This does not mean that the Revelation of God can be read directly off the pages of the historical Scriptures, for the actuality of Revelation is only indirectly identical with the actuality of the Bible . . . It is because we cannot speak of a direct identity of the Scripture as such with Revelation, although we cannot separate the Scripture from that Revelation, that our knowledge of the Bible as the Word of God is itself an event, an ever-new breaking-through to Revelation of faith and obedience.

It is important, then, to recognize that in the Bible there is this 'wall' between us and divine Revelation, namely, the man-conditioned and time-conditioned character of the witness. If we deny or ignore it, then we turn the Bible into an organ of direct and immediate oracular communication, and, in point of fact, deny Revelation itself, that is, deny God himself in his Revelation whom we hear and know only in decisive encounter and to whom we respond in faith and obedience.

Moreover, the word of the Christian to the non-Christian is nothing more than an indirect witness; it is impossible to give direct and unambiguous answers.

The Word of God itself cannot be broken or retracted. But our human word about God *is* broken, and only in this 'brokenness' – this absence of limpidly clear self-evidencing terms – can it bear witness to the truth of God. 'We know that we are unable to comprehend except by means of dialectical dualism, in which one must become two in order that it may be veritably one' ... 'If you ask me about God', Barth once wrote, 'If you ask me about *God*, and if I am ready to tell about him, dialectic is all that can be expected of *me*. Neither my affirmation nor my denial lays claim to being God's truth Neither is more than a *witness* to that Truth which stands in the centre between every Yes and No.' (H. R. Mackintosh)

His answer to questions about truth. How can we *know* the Word of God? How can we *know* what God is saying to us? How can we be sure that it is *true*?

Barth's answer rules out the possibility of any kind of verification which is carried over from the sciences.

In the knowledge of God, we are concerned with an incomparable object (the Lord, God), and therefore it cannot be scientific to carry over from our knowledge of other objects the specific form of rationality or the specific method of knowledge science has had to develop in accordance with their (creaturely) nature. (T. F. Torrance)

He therefore refuses to discuss the pre-suppositions of the non-Christian. The following passages are from Barth's Exposition of Anselm's work *Fides Quaerens Intellectum*.

And the other possibility, the possibility of a discussion on the 'unbeliever's' ground, was for Anselm, be it 'easy' or 'difficult', excluded and forbidden – it was no possibility at all.

Thus it is concluded that his statement ('there is no God') is nonsense, must be nonsense and is debarred from serious theological debate.

Perhaps Anselm did not know any other way of speaking of the Christian *Credo* except by addressing the sinner as one who had not sinned, the non-Christian as a Christian, the unbeliever as believer, on the basis of the great 'as if' which is really not an 'as if' at all, but which at all times has been the final and decisive means whereby the believer could speak to the unbeliever. Perhaps, desiring to prove, he did not really remain standing on this side of the gulf between the believer and non-believer but crossed it, though on this occasion not in search of a truce as has been said of him and has often happened, but ... as conqueror whose weapon was the fact that he met the unbelievers as one of them and accepted them as his equal.

The approach which Barth derived from this study of Anselm determined his approach from that time onwards. Thus, writing a new preface to his work on Anselm in 1958, he explains:

... in this book (*Fides Quaerens Intellectum*) on Anselm I am working with a vital key, if not the key, to an understanding of that whole process of thought that has impressed me more and more in my *Church Dogmatics* as the only one proper to theology.

In his Dogmatics, therefore, he refuses to discuss basic presuppositions like the existence of God and the possibility of revelation.

Really responsible, up-to-date theological thought, in genuine rapprochement with its contemporaries, will reveal itself to be such even today ... by refusing to discuss the basis of its ground, questions such as whether God is, whether there is such a thing as revelation, *etc*.

Thus, if we asked Barth, 'How can I know if Christianity is true?' his answer would be 'through *obedience*,' through complete surrender to the Word of God.

If faith is indeed the knowledge of the Creator then it cannot understand itself as acting creatively, but only as acting obediently. It is knowledge of the truth solely in virtue of the fact that the truth is *spoken* to us to which we respond in pure obedience.

All that man can do therefore is listen and be informed, and then say 'yes':

In his dialectical thinking Barth was faced with a fundamental problem of all theology and all thinking about God. It is *man* who thinks, *man* who asks searching questions about God, *man* who is hungry to know God, to speak about him, and make judgements about him; but when that man stands face to face with God, he discovers that he stands at the bar of *God's* judgement and it is *God* who speaks to him and questions him. Man begins by investigating God but discovers that God is all the time investigating him – and when he tries to express that, theologically, he finds that all his grammar gets upset – for God is always indissolubly Subject – and all he can do is to stammer 'yes' and 'no' in very fragmentary utterances. 'I believe; help thou my unbelief.'

Barth recognizes that there is an element of question-begging in this approach. But he believes that the method of theology is such that we have no alternative to this kind of procedure.

We know God only through God and in God, or in that we are known by him, and therefore we cannot offer any proof of our knowledge of God outside of our actual knowledge of him, that is, outside of our acknowledgement of his self-revelation. We cannot offer any evidence of our knowledge of God's Word, except in that we recognize that Word in its self-evidence to us and participate in its communication. But does that not mean that we both start from God as our presupposition and end with him as our conclusion, that we are really moving in a circle?

Barth admits that, looked at from the point of view of logical form, that is a *petitio principii* ... but the question must be asked whether in a genuine *theo*-logy we are not shut up to this kind of movement by the very nature of the subject-matter, that is, by the very nature of God himself? That is indeed the case, for in the knowledge of God we are concerned with One who is his own ground and his own evidence, and knowledge of this God can take place only as he breaks into the midst of our knowing of this world, to give us knowledge of himself beyond any possibility of our own.

PROBLEMS AND QUESTIONS

 **One can never be sure the words mean what they say**

Both Christians and non-Christians have pointed out that one basic problem with this answer is that one can never be sure one can take any form of words about Christian beliefs at their face value.

Stephen Neill:

One of the more valid criticisms of the Barthian position is that Barth has never succeeded in making quite clear what he does mean by the phrase 'the Word of God'.

William Warren Bartley, writing about Barth's approach:

All theological statements ... are for ever *conjectures* about the Word of God. We can never know whether or not our statements do in fact express the truth about the Word of God or whether they are mixed with error stemming from our misinterpretations, from our conscious or unconscious imposition of our own presuppositions on the historical event.

and about Bultmann:

... is this existentialism more than nominally theistic? Bultmann's pupil Kamlah took the final step of pointing out that what Bultmann takes the life of faith to be makes its possibility logically independent of the occurrence of any event in Palestine in the first century and, indeed, of the existence of a supernatural being. Christianity is secularized by stages into an atheistic philosophy. Bultmann's own retention of some elements of traditional Christian theism appears to have no rational jurisdiction within the framework of his own thought.

The non-Christian has every right to protest if he is conscious of any dishonesty or calculated ambiguity.

C. E. M. Joad, writing to Arnold Lunn about Christian interpretations of the Genesis account of creation and his own loss of faith:

The process of disillusionment once begun went

far and fast. I discovered that many of the Bible stories were untrue, and that science, supported by an impressive weight of evidence and backed up by the plain facts of experience, required us to suppose that many events had taken place quite otherwise than the Bible recorded. I saw that the Church treated this evidence dishonestly, first denying it and, when it could deny it no longer, affirming that it had no bearing upon the truths of Christianity, which being spiritual, belonged to a sphere other than that of science. The statements once presented to me in 'Scripture' as constituting a record of historical facts were, it now appeared, of spiritual significance only. Or weren't they? To this day I do not know. But perhaps you will enlighten me affirming on what principle you know the story of the Resurrection to be history and of the Creation myth.

Beatrice Webb:

I am aware that these dogmas (*e.g.* of the virgin birth and the resurrection of Jesus) are considered by some practising Christians to be not statements of fact at all, but merely symbols of some invisible truth – appeals to the emotion and not to the intellect. This gloss on the creed of Christendom seems to me lacking in candour.

When we compare the statements of some theologians with the statements of those who make no profession of Christian faith, it often turns out that they are saying precisely the same thing.

Colin Wilson sees no objection to using Christian language to convey his own kind of humanism:

Of Christianity, the Outsider would state that every one of its doctrines has two meanings: the idea of Christ the Redeemer, Heaven and Hell, original sin, can be understood in the obvious physical sense – the sense in which most Christians have always understood them – and a spiritual sense, which is as elusive to the ordinary person as the Invisible man. The obvious physical sense appears to the Outsider as no better than a fabrication of myths and fairy-tales; but the spiritual sense remains true.

. . Jesus' aim was the aim of every prophet and artist – to make men *more alive*, more conscious; a desire to get more life and more Will out of a great sea of half-dead monsters . . . This, then, is the essence of Christ's teaching: it is the will of the life-force that men should strive for more consciousness and life (or, as Jesus would have expressed it, it is God's will that men strive to become more like him).

If the language of the Christian does not mean what it says, then the ordinary man can be forgiven if he reacts as Alice reacts to the word-juggling and evasiveness of Humpty Dumpty:

'When *I* use a word,' Humpty Dumpty said in rather a scornful tone, 'it means just what I choose it to mean – neither more nor less.'
'The question is,' said Alice, 'whether you *can* make words mean different things.'
'The question is,' said Humpty Dumpty, 'which is to be master – that's all . . . '
'When I make a word do a lot of work like that,' said Humpty Dumpty, 'I always pay it extra' . . .

Alice waited a minute to see if he would speak again, but as he never opened his eyes or took any further notice of her, she said 'Good-bye!' once more, and, on getting no answer to this, she quietly walked away: but she could not help saying to herself as she went 'Of all the unsatisfactory – . . of all the unsatisfactory people I *ever* met – ' She never finished the sentence . . .

Faith is not open to verification in the ordinary sense

This kind of answer amounts to an invitation to take a blind leap of faith. For when the Christian is challenged by the unbeliever, he seems to retreat into a private stronghold, putting up a notice saying 'FAITH – PRIVATE'. He seems to be saying, 'You can't catch me! My faith is purely personal and inward; it has nothing to do with reason or science. You cannot prove or disprove it.'

If the Christian is more positive and tries to persuade the non-Christian to believe on the basis of this kind of answer, his invitation sounds in effect like this: 'I can't point to any evidence to convince you that Christian beliefs are true. You have simply got to believe them by an act of faith. You must have the experience of faith yourself. Simply commit yourself. Launch out in faith. There is no completely convincing evidence I can offer you, and in any case, evidence is unnecessary or irrelevant. Simply believe! The only certainty that is possible will be found after you have committed yourself in faith.'

T. W. Fowle (writing in 1881):

The time is then, I think, rapidly drawing on when modern thought will demand of theology, and that with some excusable peremptoriness of tone, to state once for all upon which footing it elects to stand. At present the tone of many scientific minds seems to be somewhat as follows: 'We really cannot occupy ourselves in serious discussion, because we never quite know where we have you. You always seem to us to assume a supernatural standpoint, and then, when confronted with obvious difficulties involved in this, to fly elsewhere for refuge. Adopt the alternative that it is only a framework for moral ideas and spiritual truths, and that too we can make shift to estimate. But to halt uneasily between the two, and to say that so tremendous an event as the resurrection of a dead man may

have happened or may not, but that on the whole it does not much matter, is to impose a fatal barrier to sincere discussion with minds that have been trained to estimate the nature and consequences of fact. If this story be true, then every conception that man can form of himself and his surroundings must be carefully modified; if it be false, then it should not be allowed to intrude itself upon a religion which, as more than half seem to assure us, having first succeeded in convincing themselves, was not founded upon it, does not need it, and would be better without it.

Colin Wilson, writing about an illustration from Jean-Paul Sartre:

If the phone rang, and a voice at the other end said: 'This is God speaking. Believe and you are saved; doubt and you are damned,' the man holding the receiver would be justified in answering: 'Very well, in that case I'm damned.' He would be justified because all men have a right to withhold belief in something they cannot know.

Marghanita Laski:

It is thoroughly depressing to learn ... that some people can argue that 'man is part of an evolving consciousness in Nature', and that in death the 'hallmark' of evolution is carried into another dimension. What conceivable sense or use could stem from such propositions, and in any case how could they be shown to be true or false?

William Warren Bartley:

The leading Protestant theologians of the twentieth century have ... embraced as fact the philosophical contention that rationality is logically limited, that every man – wil he, nil he, makes some ultimately irrational commitment; and they have used this contention to excuse rationally their own irrational commitment to Christ. Thereby, they have been able in principle, although not in practice, to avoid loss of intellectual integrity.

My basic objection to Barth's thought ... involves the absolute irrational commitment on which he bases his theory ...

For many of us the difficulty lies in the initial irrational assumption. We wish to question the truth of the Word of God. And that in itself puts us outside Barth's Church.

Leslie Newbiggin writing about John Oman and Barth:

He (Oman) was more aware than many theologians are of the ease with which theology can become dishonest. He insisted on asking at every point the question: 'How do you know?' It is one of the accidents of history that his greatest book, *The Natural and the Supernatural* ... appeared just at the time when the rise of Barthian theology was sweeping that question under the carpet.

J. S. Bezzant, writing about Bultmann:

No intelligent person desires to substitute prudent acceptance of the demonstrable for faith; but when I am told that it is precisely its immunity from proof which secures the Christian proclamation from the charge of being mythological,

I reply that immunity from proof can 'secure' nothing whatever except immunity from proof, and call nonsense by its proper name. Nor do I think that anything like historical Christianity can be relieved of objections by making the validity of assertions depend upon the therapeutic function it plays in healing fractures in the souls of believers, or understand how it can ever have this healing function unless it can be believed to be true.

The approach which suggests that one should simply preach Christ and leave questions about presuppositions on one side in the hope that the proclamation of Christ will lead to faith in God, is likely to become more and more unrealistic and ineffective in the agnostic world of today where the Christian is surrounded by a non-Christian majority. The mere preaching of Christ is no substitute for talking about questions of truth, God and man, and the universe.

Altizer:

Christ cannot appear as God at the time in which God is dead.

Ninian Smart:

Christ's claims are not self-authenticating. There are ... certain presuppositions which have to be accepted before the claims can be substituted as they stand. And these presuppositions will be repudiated by Jews and Muslims, to mention no others.

This exchange between *Alice* and the Queen reminds us of the natural reaction to any invitation to believe what is unreasonable or impossible:

'Let's consider your age to begin with – how old are you?'
'I'm seven and a half exactly.'
'You needn't say "exactly",' the Queen remarked: 'I can believe it without that. Now I'll give *you* something to believe. I'm just one hundred and one, five months and a day.'
'I can't believe *that*!' said Alice.
'Can't you?' the Queen said in a pitying voice. 'Try again: draw a long breath, and shut your eyes.'
Alice laughed. 'There's no use trying,' she said: 'one *can't* believe impossible things.'
'I daresay you haven't had much practice,' said the Queen. 'When I was your age, I always did it for half-an-hour every day. Why, sometimes I've believed as many as six impossible things before breakfast!'

6. THE ANSWER OF MYSTICISM

"We can know Christianity is true only through mystical experience"

The mystical approach to truth holds that we cannot hope to be able to verify Christian beliefs, or to demonstrate by reason that they are true, or simply to feel in the heart that they are true. We can only hope to know through mystical experience.

David Knowles writes that mystical theology claims to be:

an incommunicable and inexpressible knowledge and love of God or of religious truth received in the spirit without precedent, effort or reasoning.

F. C. Happold gives this summary of the main characteristics of mystical states:

1. They defy expression in terms which are fully intelligible to those who have not had some analogous experience.
2. Though states of feeling, they are also states of knowledge, resulting in a deeper insight into the nature of things.
3. Except in the case of true contemplatives, when they can result in a permanent shift of consciousness, they are infrequent and of short duration.
4. They convey the sense of something 'given', not dependent on one's own volition.
5. There is a consciousness of the oneness of everything.
6. They also have a sense of timelessness.
7. There is forced on one the conviction that the familiar phenomenal *ego* is not the real *I*.

The same writer believes that the religion of the future must be a mystical religion:

The whole of our analysis more and more forces us to the conclusion that the *only possible religion for twentieth-century man is a mystical religion and that all theological language must be recognized as a language of symbols.*

H. R. Rookmaaker in his book *Modern Art and the Death of a Culture* says:

There is no age as mystical as ours. Yet it is mysticism with a difference: it is a nihilistic mysticism, for God is dead. Very old ideas are being revived: gnosticism, neo-platonic ideas of reality emanating from and returning to God, and Eastern religion, a religion with a god that is not a god but impersonal and universalist, a god which (not who!) is everything and therefore nothing, with a salvation that is in the end self-annihilation. In the quest for humanity man is even willing to lose his identity, his personality. It is like the creed that the Beatles sing (on their Sergeant Pepper Lonely Hearts Club Band record): 'When you've seen beyond yourself . . . the time will come when you see we're all one and life flows on within you and without you.'

Mystical experience is said to lead to a real knowledge of 'the truth' about the universe. This truth is inexpressible in words, but it can be felt. The medium can be music, drugs, meditation, or the traditional observance of eastern religious faiths.

Albert Ayler, a leader of the new wave in jazz of 1965:

Music is a prayer, a message from God, it is freedom, beyond the material.

Brian Wilson, the Beach Boys:

My experience of God came from Acid; its the most important thing that's ever happened to me.

A member of the Divine Light Mission, followers of 14-year-old *Guru Maharaj Ji:*

When your mind is still, then this truth will come up inside you. And really stillness of mind, which brings peace, is what everybody's looking for . . . when you stop thinking and just start experiencing . . . It's not a bad thing to think, but really if you want the eternal truth you reach a state of thoughtlessness . . . There's only one proof with spiritual truth: you'll know when you've got what you want.

Aldous Huxley:

Meditation is more than a method of self-education; it has also been used, in every part of the world and from the remotest periods, as a method for acquiring knowledge about the essential nature of things, a method for establishing communion between the soul and the integrating principle of the universe. Meditation, in other words, is the technique of mysticism . . . Properly practised . . . meditation may result in a state of what has been called 'transcendental consciousness'—the direct intuition of, and union with an ultimate spiritual reality that is perceived as simultaneously beyond the self and in some way within it.

Many of those involved in the world of the popular arts are expressing the change such experiences have made to their whole generation's view of reality:

Brian Wilson, the Beach Boys:

Then things began changing in my personal life. A whole tide of miracles was basically altering my whole generation. I completely blew my mind. For a while I wasn't myself at all. It was good. I started approaching my music-making as an art-form—something pure from the spirit to which I could add dynamics and marketable reality. I'm very aware of the value and power of

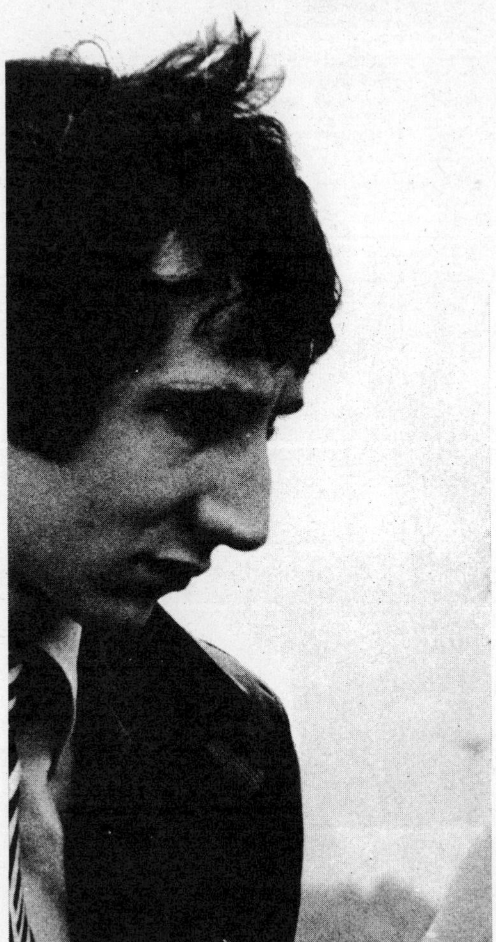

Peter Townsend of The Who pop group.

speaking through a song. Not messages—just what you can say through music itself.

Larry Ramos, of the Association:

And you know this awareness you were talking about, well, I know a lot of people who are involved in various forms of mysticism at various levels . . . and it's all part of the same thing. We're going through fantastic changes. Like me, I thought I was a real atheist . . . But, believe me, it's something else now. It's like we created our own church; the church of kids.

Peter Townsend, the Who:

The simple point is that I believe in the probability of anything, including flying saucers. That's only possible if you believe in cosmic power.

BUDDHISM

Buddhism, especially as it is in the school of Zen, aims at a mystical experience which, it is claimed, brings real knowledge.

Christmas Humphreys:

The purpose of Zen is to pass beyond the intellect. All that we know, we know but about. The expert, a wit has said, learns more and more about less and less; Zen wearies of learning about it and about, and strives to *know*. For this a new faculty is needed, the power of immediate perception, the intuitive awareness which comes when the perceiver and the perceived are merged in one. All mystics use this faculty, and all alike are unable to make their knowledge known. But he who knows can only say that he knows; to communicate what he knows he has to descend to the realm of concepts, counters of agreed and common meaning. Such are words, but they are fallible means of making our knowledge known . . . What *knows*? The answer is Buddhi, the faculty of direct awareness, as present in every human mind as the intellect which all possess but few have yet developed to the full.

All phrases, dogmas, formulas; all schools and codes; all systems of thought and philosophy, all 'isms', including Buddhism, all these are means to the end of *knowing*, and easily become and are not perceived as obstacles in the way. Zen technique is designed to develop the mind to the limits of thought and then to drive it to the verge of the precipice, where thought can go no further. And then? As Dr Graham Howe, the psychiatrist, often says to his patients, 'when you come to a precipice, why stop, or go round, or go back? Why not go over?' For only then can we go on, and progress is a walking on and on to the Goal. It is true that at a later stage one learns that there is no walking and no Goal, but that is Zen . . . Meanwhile, until we achieve the goal of purposelessness, let us have this purpose: Said the Master Ummon to his monks, 'If you walk, just walk; if you sit, just sit, but don't wobble!' . . .

The vision may come quite suddenly or slowly arise. It is in no way to be confused with a psychic trance or the phantasy of the schizophrenic. Nor is it concerned with morality or any man-made code. It is a foretaste of the Absolute Moment, of Cosmic Consciousness, of the condition in which I and my Father are one . . .

. . . Others who have tried to describe the reward of their years of tremendous effort speak of a sense of certainty, of serenity, of clarity, and of unity with nature and the universe around. Hui-neng described the serenity:

> Imperturbable and serene the ideal man
> practises no virtue;
> Self-possessed and dispassionate he commits
> no sin;
> Calm and silent he gives up seeing and hearing;
> Even and upright his mind abides nowhere.

PROBLEMS AND QUESTIONS

 **Mysticism is founded on extreme agnosticism and is open to all the same objections**

The mystic seeks for his experience because he has despaired of finding the truth through the other approaches. He believes that all the other approaches lead not to knowledge but to profound ignorance.

Dionysius the Areopagite:

. . . neither does anything that is, know Him as He is; . . . neither can the reason attain to Him, nor name Him, nor know Him; neither is He darkness, nor light, nor the false nor the true; nor can any affirmation or negation be applied to Him, for though we may affirm or deny the things below Him, we can neither affirm nor deny Him, inasmuch as the all-perfect and unique Cause of all things transcends all affirmation, and the simple pre-eminence of His absolute nature is outside of every negation—free from every limitation beyond them all.

Aldous Huxley:

To the mystics who are generally regarded as the best of their kind, ultimate reality . . . appears as a spiritual reality so far beyond particular form or personality that nothing can be predicated of it.

'The atman is silence' is what the Hindus say of ultimate spiritual reality. The only language that can convey any idea about the nature of this reality is the language of negation, of paradox, of extravagant exaggeration. The pseudo-Dionysius speaks of the 'ray of the divine darkness' of 'the super-lucent darkness of silence' and of the necessity to 'leave behind the senses and the intellectual operations and all things known by sense and intellect'. 'If anyone', he writes, 'seeing God, understands what he has seen, he has not seen God.' 'Nescio, nescio,' was what St Bernard wrote of the ultimate reality; 'neti, neti,' was Yajnavalkya's verdict at the other side of the world. 'I know not, I know not: not so, not so.'

The mystical approach is therefore open to the same objections as the approach of agnosticism. (See pp. 50–59)

For example, the mystic is prepared to hold together opposites. His utterances are not subject to the laws of logic. He can hold two contradictory beliefs together at the same time.

Nicholas of Cusa:

I have learnt that the place where Thou (*i.e.* God) art found unveiled is girt round with the co-incidence of contradictories, and this is the wall of Paradise wherein Thou dost abide, the door whereof is guarded by the proud spirit of Reason, and, unless he is vanquished, the way will not be open. Thus 'tis beyond the coincidence of contradictories Thou mayest be seen and nowhere this side thereof.

Simone Weil:

The mysteries of the faith are not a proper object of the intelligence, permitting affirmation or denial. They are not of the order of truth, but are above it. The only part of the human soul which is capable of any real contact with them is the faculty of supernatural Love. It alone therefore is capable of an adherence in regard to them.

This can lead, therefore, to a synthesis of contradictory ideas and of religious beliefs of many different religions and philosophies:

F. C. Happold:

We are thus led on to draw a distinction between *Truth* and *truths*. Each partial *truth* may be true within its own sphere, but be only a fragment of *Truth* in its fullness; and, owing to the limitations of human perception, there is not seldom a conflict between different *truths*.

To India was given the vision of the spiritual foundation of the universe and the immanence of God in it; to Palestine the vision of the significance of the material world and of the historical process; to Greece the vision of order and reason.

Each of these visions of reality can be seen as complementary, each as a fragment of the full truth, each supplementing the other. All are necessary if one is to grasp the full significance of the Christ . . . .

If you have stood in a Buddhist temple and gazed up at a beautiful statue of the Buddha above the flower-decked altar, you cannot, if you are spiritually sensitive, but have been impressed by the calm serenity of the face gazing down on you. This was the teacher who taught the way of the ending of the world's sorrow and an all-embracing compassion towards every sentient being. Here before you is the Buddhist 'God-image'. And, as you gazed, there may have come before you another symbol, another God-image, the image of the Man of Sorrows who took upon himself the world's sorrow and showed forth the love of God on a cross on a desolate hill. Are the two images incompatible; or are they complementary; two sides of the face of the Divine Totality?

Members of the Hari Krishna movement, in their yellow robes, have become familiar figures in London and New York shopping streets.

The knowledge gained through mystical experience can only be expressed in symbol and myth

F. C. Happold:

We are . . . compelled to use the only language available, a language of symbol and paradox, which may be alien and incomprehensible to one not accustomed to it. The Divine Ground can be spoken of only in a language of polarity, a language of opposites, as non-personal and personal, supranatural and transnatural, other and not-other, without and within, transcendent and immanent, as Eternal Rest and yet evolving activity. All these descriptions are true in their different spheres and at their different levels of significance and awareness. None, alone, expresses the complete truth.

But there can never be a 'true' interpretation of what a symbol means. It can mean different things to different people, and no one is in a position to say whether one person has grasped the truth more clearly than another. There is a profound ambiguity about symbols.

F. C. Happold:

We can feel that a symbol has meaning, indeed most profound meaning, yet we cannot hope to put into words exactly how or why. Not only that, symbols are ambivalent, they act differently on and convey different meanings to different people. A symbol acts on the hearer or seer in such a way that it arouses in him feelings of awe or fear or love; it shifts his centre of awareness, so that things are perceived in a different light; it changes his values. It has thus a dynamic quality.

Those who do not begin with the same assumption of extreme agnosticism are bound to react to the language of symbols with indifference or impatience:

C. E. M. Joad:

I have never been able to make anything of symbolism. A symbol I understand to be a sign for something else. Either the symbolist knows what the something else is, in which case I cannot see why he should not tell us what it is straight out, instead of obscurely hinting at it in symbols, or he does not, in which case not knowing what the symbols stand for he cannot expect his readers to find out for him. Usually, I suspect, he does not, and his symbolism is merely a device to conceal his muddled thinking.

Mystical knowledge is incommunicable apart from mystical experience

We cannot hope to know the truth until we have experienced the truth through some kind of mystical experience. And until and unless we have the experience, we cannot hope to know the truth. We cannot investigate anything with our minds first, and then decide whether we think it is true and whether we are going to commit ourselves to it. We cannot really begin to know what we are talking about until we have had the experience. And even when we ourselves have had the experience, we cannot hope to be able to describe or explain it adequately to others.

F. C. Happold, writing about mystical states:

They defy expression in terms which are fully intelligible to those who have not had some analogous experience.

C. E. M. Joad:

. . . what, after all, is the nature of the distinction between knowledge and feeling? It is that knowledge is essentially communicable, while feeling is not, precisely because knowledge is of the intellect, and reason is public and common, whereas feeling is personal and private . . . It is for precisely this reason that the testimony of mystical experience in religion carries so little weight with non-mystics, for the mystics, in seeking to convey the nature of the reality which their experience reports to them are conveying something which is strictly meaningless to those who have not themselves had experience of that reality . . .

Now the reason why knowledge is communicable and feeling is not is to be found in the fact that knowledge is of something other than and external to itself, whereas feeling reports nothing but the fact of the feeling. Knowledge, in short, involves a reference to something else, namely, that which is known; feeling does not.

BACK TO ANSWER ONE

"God has revealed the truth to man, and it is open to verification"

PROBLEMS AND QUESTIONS

Having examined other possible answers to the basic question, we must now return to option one, the Biblical Christian answer, and look at some of the main questions and objections raised.

 This approach makes no appeal to the heart or the feelings or the imagination. It presents a cold orthodoxy which is abstract and impersonal.

Renan:

A religion as clear as geometry arouses no love or hate.

S. T. Coleridge:

Evidences of Christianity! I am weary of the word. Make a man feel the *want* of it; rouse him, if you can, to the self-knowledge of his *need* of it; and you may safely trust it to its own Evidence.

Ronald Knox, the Roman Catholic apologist, suggests that the task of the Christian apologist is to:

suggest to the reader that in approaching Christian theology he is approaching something that is alive, not a series of diagrams. The hardest part of the author's task . . . will be to introduce some human element into natural theology; to prove that God is, and what God is, not merely with the effect of intellectual satisfaction, but with a glow of assent that springs from the whole being; 'did not our hearts burn within us when he talked with us by the way?'

But his task will not end there . . . He will prove the divineness of our Lord's mission, not by presenting us with a series of logical dilemmas, but by trying to reconstruct the picture of our Lord himself, what it was that met the gaze of the Apostles, and the touch of their hands. He will read the New Testament not as a set of 'passages' which must somehow be reconciled with one another, but as the breathless confidences of living men, reacting to human situations, and inflamed with zeal for their Master . . . Everything will come alive at his touch; he will not merely know what he is talking about, but feel what he is talking about.

▷ If we are prepared to accept the biblical understanding of truth, there is no need to drive a wedge between 'the logical dilemmas' and the 'human element' in the way Knox does. They need not be mutually exclusive. It need not be a case of *either/or*. One way to introduce 'some human element' into natural theology is to show a real awareness of what it *feels* like to live consistently in a universe without God. And in contrast to this, one can then reconsider what it *feels* like to live in the Christian universe on the basis of what God has revealed.

H. E. Root:

If the gospel is to be communicated in any form, it must be commended by those with an imaginative awareness of its alternatives.

▷ Some Christian apologists have made great appeal to the imagination: *e.g.* George Macdonald and C. S. Lewis.

Alec Vidler sums up the strength of C. S. Lewis as an apologist in this way:

As a Christian apologist, Lewis was primarily an imaginative writer. In the midst of a culture dominated by science, technology and a secular outlook, he somehow managed to convey a sense of the reality of an invisible, eternal realm of being to which this world is subordinate. Words like heaven and hell, glory and guilt, redemption and miracle, the transcendent and the supernatural, which have become dead or archaic for most people nowadays, and to which it often seems that Christians pay no more than lip-service, in his hands acquire substance and fascination.

But there is a vast difference between the world of C. S. Lewis's books and the fantasy world of, for example, the Beatles' film *The Yellow Submarine*:

Roll up, roll up! Come for a magical mystery ride with the Beautiful Beatles, far, far away to Pepperland . . . Travel with Old Fred and the Beatles as they journey in their yellow submarine through strange seas, peopled with dream characters, and find the realms beyond reality. Enter the colourful cartoon world of the Beatles' newest journey into fantasy . . .

They have to sail through eight seas until they eventually reach the underwater Pepperland. Each sea has a name and different hazards to be encountered. There are the Seas of Time, Music, Science, Consumer Products, Nowhere, Monsters, Green Phrenology and Holes, and the weird assortment of characters encountered including Shakespeare, Queen Elizabeth, the U.S. Cavalry, Napoleon, Einstein, Freud, King Kong, Paul's clean old grandad . . . cowboys, Indians, Father MacKenzie from 'Eleanor Rigby', the Sheik, Cicero, Lucy (In the Sky with Diamonds, of course) and the Boob, who is a sheep-like creature with a large nose, and who represents 'Nowhere Man' . . .

The outlook behind a film of this kind takes as its starting-point answers 4 or 6 to the question of truth (see pp. 47 and 74). The books of C. S. Lewis are therefore not likely to communicate the Christian message to a person who accepts the outlook of this kind of film, unless he realizes that Lewis uses his imaginary world not only to entertain but to say things about the *real* world. Anyone who knows Lewis's beliefs from his straightforward apologetic books can understand without much difficulty what the different stories signify in terms of the real world.

▷ It is certainly true that the Christian faith is often presented in a coldly orthodox and abstract way. But there is no reason why it should be.

The following extract from *Constance Padwick's* biography of Temple Gairdner of Cairo shows how one Christian apologist in the world of Islam was aware of the problem and how he tried to solve it himself:

Gairdner . . . found that the literature by which the Christian Church had set forth her living truth to Moslems was a curiously arid, machine-made literature. It was as though the compilers, holy men though they were, had been caught into the argumentative machinery of the schoolmen, and had expended all their vital strength in meeting Moslem arguments with juster arguments. The objector himself might be left on the field prostrate but cursing. The books were starved of personality and of appeal to aught save logic and justice. Moreover he saw, and it was one of his most fruitful perceptions, that the converts made by this literature were often born in its image—with the spirit of disputation rather than worship and of love, and apt to hammer rather than to woo and win.

Gairdner believed . . . that there must needs be an apologetic literature, unafraid of controversial points. Silence, he felt, was tantamount to denial of the truth he knew and lived. But the literature must be humanized and written for fellow-men, not only for the defeat of argufiers. Moreover, to Gairdner, stories, history, drama, music, poetry, pictures, all that could bear the impress of the Spirit of Christ, was a reasonable part of the Christian apologetic to the whole man. . .

'We need the *song* note in our message to the Moslems . . . not the dry cracked note of disputation, but the song of joyous witness, tender invitation.'

▷ This objection is sometimes based on a fundamentally different understanding of truth—*e.g.* that truth can be discerned only by the heart or the feelings, or by a leap of faith. This assumption is specially evident, for example, in Coleridge, who makes Reason and Faith totally different from each other.

 **This approach makes no appeal to the conscience; there is no challenge to repentance**

This is how *Emil Brunner* voices his protest against the perversion of the Christian message into a 'sterile orthodoxy':

Faith has become doctrine, a matter for the intellect, a play of thought, scholasticism . . . Dogma, the merely intellectual expression of the divine truth in Christ has itself become deified. The fact that God's Word is not a static theory, that it is not a Word which man can manipulate as he chooses, but that it is a living personal challenge has become forgotten . . . The word is no longer a challenge; it has become an object for consideration, a theory.

▷ The Biblical approach we have outlined should not involve any softening down of the ultimate challenge to repentance. But the crucial point at issue is: what do we say when the unbeliever (or the believer) asks, 'How can I *know* if this gospel is true? How can I repent before God if I cannot be sure that he is there or that Jesus is the person he claims to be?' According to Brunner, however, when the Christian is asked questions of this kind, he is under no obligation to answer them; for it is the unbeliever who should be putting forward reasons for not believing (see p. 60).

The approach we have outlined is based on the assumption that we have every right to ask questions of this kind *and* to expect substantial answers. If we are in earnest in asking our questions, we will soon realize that we are not simply doing intellectual exercises or playing games with words.

⚠ People are not as rational as they think they are

This objection, at least in its modern form, can be traced back primarily to Freud's psychological determinism, which says that all our 'rational' thinking is little more than rationalizations of what is hidden in the subconscious mind. All our reasoning is determined by factors of which we are hardly aware. Our decisions are influenced by instinct and feeling rather than by reason and logic.

Freud sums up his attitude to religion in these words:

While the different religions wrangle with one another as to which of them is in possession of the truth, in our view the truth of religion may be altogether disregarded. Religion is an attempt to get control over the sensory world, in which we are placed, by means of the wish-world, which we have developed inside us as a result of biological and psychological necessities. But it cannot achieve its end. Its doctrines carry with them the stamp of the times in which they originated, the ignorant childhood days of the human race. Its consolations deserve no trust. Experience teaches us that the world is not a nursery. The ethical commands, to which religion seeks to lend its weight, require some other foundation instead, for human society cannot do without them, and it is dangerous to link up obedience to them with religious beliefs. If one attempts to assign to religion its place in man's evolution, it seems not so much to be a lasting acquisition as a parallel to the neurosis which the civilized individual must pass through on his way from childhood to maturity.

Leslie Paul writes about the effect of Freud's teaching in this way:

Freud's concept of the unconscious is probably the most revolutionary change in thought which this century has produced . . . The acceptance of the existence of the unconscious struck a blow at a fundamental humanist principle—the rationality of the mind. If the mind was subject to occult influences, never properly exposed to reason, let alone controlled by it, and if these occult influences determined to some extent the structure of the mind—what indeed became of the supremacy of human reason and therefore of the sovereignty of man?

This way of thinking is now so widely accepted that it is assumed everyone recognizes its truth:

Colin Wilson:

Is modern man justified in believing in God on the basis of faith? There is, of course, no simple answer to this simple question; in the final analysis it appears to be more a question of emotional motivation than of rational argument.

Ann Jellico:

When I write a play I am trying to communicate with the audience. I do this by every means in my power— I try to get at them through their eyes, by providing visual action; I try to get at them through their ears, for instance by noises and rhythm . . . I am trying to use every possible effect that the theatre can offer to stir up the audience—to get at them through their emotions . . . I write this way because—the image everybody has of the rational, intellectual and intelligent man—I don't believe it's true. I think people are driven by their emotions, and by their fears and insecurities.

▷ The objection does at least admit that Christian beliefs do seem to meet certain human needs we all feel, *e.g.* the need to find some meaning and purpose in life. But the Christian is not ashamed that these beliefs meet his need any more than he is ashamed to eat food because it meets his physical need. The fact that these beliefs meet a need does not by itself prove they must be false.

▷ The Christian does not deny that heredity and environment have a very important influence on all our beliefs and decisions. But he would deny that these factors (even if we could understand them completely) account for *every* belief and decision. He does so on the basis of his belief that man can make certain genuinely free choices because he bears something of the image of the God who can act in perfect freedom.

▷ Psychological determinism has serious effects on personal relationships. It means that we cannot take other people at face value; instead we are always trying to find out what makes the other person speak and act in the way he does.

▷ If this kind of determinism is completely consistent, then there is no place left for any free choices or for the free acceptance of any beliefs. But we all live on the assumption that we are genuinely free in certain ways—*e.g.* we assume we are free to decide whether or not to read to the end of this page. But if all our choices and all our beliefs are determined and programmed by factors which are outside our control, then our feeling of freedom is an illusion. If we then go on living *as if* we have some freedom, we are being thoroughly inconsistent.

▷ The objector who uses these arguments from psychology to justify his rejection of Christian beliefs must allow the same kind of argument to be used against his own beliefs. This means that his rejection of God is purely and simply an expression of his feelings and his desires. If beliefs are merely the product of the subconscious, then *no one*, believer or non-believer, has the right to claim that his beliefs are *true*; all one can do is to speak about one's own feelings. But the objector imagines he enjoys a specially privileged position, and has access to objective knowledge which is denied to the Christian. He 'knows' that beliefs are motivated by the unconscious. But how can he possibly 'know' if *all* beliefs are motivated by the subconscious? If Christian beliefs are the projection of human desires and feelings, then so are his own. In this case, we must give up hope of finding the truth.

 **Is there not a basic difference between faith and knowledge? Are there not many different kinds of knowledge and certainty?**

At the risk of over-simplification we may say that the relationship between faith and knowledge can be described in three different ways. Each of them can be illustrated diagrammatically.

▷ Scientific knowledge and religious faith are *entirely different*. There is an absolute distinction between them. They belong to completely different worlds.

FAITH

———

REASON

This position was first stated by Aquinas, and was stated in its most extreme form by Kierkegaard.

Colin Wilson completely accepts this dichotomy between objective and scientific truth on the one hand and subjective, religious truth on the other:

Our criterion has been this: that any 'truth' of religion shall be determinable *subjectively*. When we normally speak of the truth of an idea, we mean that it corresponds with some outside fact. 'Truth is subjectivity', Kierkegaard said. That is the Existential concept. 'The dog is blue'. Is that, *could* it be, a religious truth? No; even if it is objectively true that the dog is blue, it is an objective truth; therefore it could not be a religious truth. 'There is a spirit world where we all go when we die.' That may be true, in the same sense that the dog is blue; but in that case it is a truth about the external world, and not therefore a religious truth.

▷ Scientific knowledge and personal knowledge are *at different ends of the same scale*. Scientific knowledge has to do with what can be measured, and is articulate knowledge. Some of our knowledge of other people comes into this category. But at the other end of the scale we have the knowledge of persons which is inarticulate. Christian faith is more like personal knowledge; it is knowledge of a Person.

Scientific knowledge —articulate and precise:	Personal knowledge —inarticulate; knowledge through involvement and interest:
<———————————————————>	
e.g. I know that this tree is 30 years old; I know that *x* is 30 years old and that he wears glasses.	*e.g.* I know what *x* is like as a person, because I have lived and worked with him for many years.

John Habgood:

We know different facets of our experience in different ways and with different degrees of precision. There is a hierarchy of knowledge. At one end of the scale there is precise scientific knowledge of those features of experience which can be treated as objects existing independently of us; at the other end, there is the knowledge we have of other persons by our involvement with them, the kind of knowledge we can only have when we *stop* treating them as objects. At one end of the scale we have extreme articulateness; at the other end, extreme inarticulateness. And just as there is an inverse relationship between articulateness and involvement, so there is also a relationship between involvement and interest. When we stop thinking about knowledge in the abstract, we have to admit that what interests us most is what involves us most as persons. Quite apart from every other consideration, a world of which we only had precise scientific knowledge would be appallingly dull.

Religious knowledge belongs to the inarticulate end of the scale and the kind of mystery which should concern it is therefore the mystery of our involvement with persons.

New Dutch Catechism:

Man has difficult steps to take before he arrives at faith . . . The first difficulty is undoubtedly the desire to be master of all things, to subject everything to our will, including man himself. There is no room for admiration or reverence. The one thing we ask is: what is there in it for me? There is no mystery about things to make us pause reverently and ask: where do they come from? We simply work out how we can be safe and try for that. The unexpected or incalculable is taboo.

Our attitude to men is the same . . . We manipulate men and things and are blind to their mystery.

. . . Covetousness, cold and hard, often mixed with pride, is a disability which lies deep in all of us, no matter how friendly we may be in our contacts.

This is a threshold which we cross when we take the step of really loving . . . We cease to calculate and foresee everything. We now see that the only way to know the other as he is is to let oneself be won over, to give oneself, to trust, to believe. Without belief there is no love. This belief in the other is not a lower form of knowledge but a higher. It is the one way of knowing the greatest thing on earth: another person . . .

If these approaches were to take seriously the comparison between Christian faith and knowledge and love of persons, they would allow a greater place for words and questions and answers in the process of finding out if Christianity is true. The process of getting to know another person – and even the process of falling in love – depends to quite a considerable extent on listening to what the other person says and asking questions to find out what he feels and thinks. It may be hard in the end to sum up exhaustively in words, our knowledge or love of another person; but if we could not use words, we could not hope to arrive at this knowledge or this love in the first place. Personal trust and love are always open to tests of various kinds and are never completely blind.

▷ There are *many different levels of certainty* in any field; but we should think of *truth and knowledge as being one and not many*. Knowledge in one area is not of a completely different kind from knowledge in another. There should be no fundamental distinction between knowledge and faith. The different levels of certainty in different areas can be illustrated by a series of parallel scales:

	PEOPLE	CHRISTIAN FAITH	SCIENCE
CERTAIN	that x and y are legally married; that x and y are utterly trustworthy and I can trust them implicitly.	that Jesus rose from the dead; that Jesus is wholly trustworthy, and that we can take him at his word.	that when water is heated to a certain temperature at a given pressure, it will boil; that dinosaurs existed.
PROBABLE	that x is deeply in love with y.	that the resurrection of Jesus is to be dated April, AD 30.	that a cure for cancer will be found.

POSSIBLE	that *x* and *y* will have twins; that *x* may let me down in small things.	that the second coming of Jesus will take place in our lifetime.	that a black cock and a black hen will produce a brown chick.
IMPROBABLE	that *x* and *y* will have quads; that *x* will become a millionaire.	that Jesus ever travelled outside Palestine.	that the Loch Ness Monster exists; that there is human life on the planets.
	∨	∨	∨

The New Testament refuses to draw a sharp line between faith and knowledge:

Simon Peter answered him, 'Lord, to whom shall we go? You have the words of eternal life; and we have *believed*, and have come to know, that you are the Holy One of God.'

His disciples said, 'Ah, now you are speaking plainly, not in any figure! Now we *know* that you know all things, and need none to question you; by this we *believe* that you came from God.'

 ## This approach deprives man of his freedom and leads to complacency

G. E. Lessing:

What constitutes man's worth is not the truth he possesses, or thinks he possesses; it is the sincerity of the effort he makes to approach it. For it is not the possession of, but the search for, truth which strengthens the forces that contribute to his evergrowing perfection. Possession makes a man easy in his mind, inert and self-satisfied. If God held the whole truth in his right hand, and in his left, the eternal longing for truth ... and if he were to bid me choose, humbly I should choose the left, saying 'Give me that, Father, for perfect truth is for thee alone.'

for the truth' to the truth itself, we must be prepared to feel the terrible pain of a thirst which will never be satisfied.

If, however, we approach the Christian faith with a desire to find the truth about it, we can ask as many questions as we want, and in the end we are utterly free to make our own decision one way or the other. And if we once believe that Christianity has the truth, there should be no complacency, but rather a longing to discover more and more of the truth, and to live by it and to demonstrate it to others.

▷ We must make our own choices and accept the consequences. If we believe that we cannot hope to understand the Riddle of Existence, then we must live with our agnosticism. And many who have tried consistently to live with their agnosticism have found that it leads not to a spirit of 'glorious adventure' but to profound despair. If we prefer 'an eternal longing

▷ There is no loss of freedom and no complacency when the believer is able to say with the psalmist:

Give me understanding, that I may keep thy law
   and observe it with my whole heart.
Open my eyes, that I may behold
   wondrous things out of thy law.

 ## Many people are not sceptical by nature and are willing to be told what the truth is

▷ It is perfectly true that some people are immediately convinced when they hear the Christian message clearly and simply explained, and when they see evidence for its

truth in the lives of other Christians. They may have no desire or no need to 'verify' Christian beliefs. But we are not justified in concluding that because *some* come to believe in this way, *all* can or ought to believe in this way.

▷ The real point at issue is whether or not we have the right to ask the question 'How can I know if Christianity is true?' This approach is based on the assumption that we *can* and *ought to* ask as many questions as we want to. If the simple Gospel story of the death and resurrection of Jesus convinces a person and speaks to his need, then he will believe without asking further questions. But there are others who want to ask more questions; like Thomas they say 'Unless . . . I will not believe.'

▷ The New Testament writers make it quite plain that when a person becomes a Christian he is meant to grow in his understanding of what he believes:

Make every effort to supplement your faith with virtue, and virtue with knowledge.

Brethren, do not be children in your thinking; be babes in evil, but in thinking be mature.

Paul prays in these terms for Christians:

We have not ceased to pray for you, asking that you may be filled with the knowledge of his will in all spiritual wisdom and understanding.

▷ Even if a person never asks 'intellectual' questions to satisfy himself before or after he becomes a Christian, he ought at least to be aware of the questions and the possible answers if he wants to be able to give an account of his faith to others:

Always be prepared to make a defence to any one who calls you to account for the hope that is in you, yet do it with gentleness and reverence.

Why so negative? Why deny so many things?

▷ In ordinary everyday speech some negatives make for greater clarity. We can often make clearer what we *do* mean by adding what we do *not* mean. For example, '*X* lives in the third house on the right; *not* the first one with the red door, and *not* the next one with black shutters, but the third one with the bird cage in the front window.'

▷ The basic rule of logic (the law of non-contradiction) says that *a* cannot be *non-a*. If I say 'this is a book', it cannot be a book and a house at the same time. If we were not able to make distinctions between things, speech would soon cease to mean very much. Negatives, therefore, help to establish that Christian beliefs are rational. We are not moving in a world in which *all* religious beliefs can be right and *none* wrong.

▷ There is a particular view of truth which says in effect that there is no need for any negatives. We need never say no to any beliefs – they can all be true. According to this view you can say,
'Jesus is a revelation of God, *and* so is Krishna, *and* so is Buddha.'
'God is personal *and* impersonal; he is kind *and* cruel.'

This is the outlook of Hinduism and of the philosophy which follows Hegel's concept of synthesis (see p. 49).
If the Christian is speaking to those who, consciously or unconsciously, accept this kind of approach, he must use some negatives if he wants to make himself understood:
'Jesus is a revelation of God; and Krishna and Buddha are *not*.'
'God is personal *and not* impersonal.'

▷ In presenting the Christian faith to the person who really understands his own culture, it is essential that the Christian should say what he accepts and what he rejects in that culture.

Bonhoeffer in this very significant passage shows how much he seems to *accept* of the assumptions of the Renaissance and of the Enlightenment:

The movement beginning about the thirteenth century . . . towards the autonomy of man (under which head I place the discovery of the laws by which the world moves and manages in science, social and political affairs, art, ethics, and religion) has in our time reached a certain completion. Man has learned to cope with all questions of importance without recourse to God as a working hypothesis. In questions concerning science, art, and even ethics, this has become an understood thing which one scarcely dares to tilt at any more. But in the last hundred years or so it has been increasingly true of religious questions also: it is becoming evident that everything gets along without 'God', and just as well as before. As in the scientific field, so in human affairs generally, what we call 'God' is being more and more edged out of life, losing more and more ground.

On the historical side I should say that there is *one* great development which leads to the idea of the autonomy of the world. In theology it is first discernible in Lord Herbert of Cherbury, with his assertion that reason is the sufficient instrument of religious knowledge. In ethics it first appears in Montaigne and Bodin with their substitution of moral principles for the ten commandments. In politics, Machiavelli, who emancipates politics from the tutelage of morality, and founds the doctrine of 'reasons of state'. Later, and very differently, though like Machiavelli tending towards the autonomy of human society, comes Grotius, with his international law as the law of nature, a law which would still be valid *etsi deus non daretur*. The process is completed in philosophy. On the one hand we have the deism of Descartes, who holds that the world is a mechanism which runs on its own without any intervention from God. On the other hand there is the pantheism of Spinoza, with its identification of God with nature. In the last resort Kant is a deist, Fichte and Hegel pantheists. All along the line there is a growing tendency to assert the autonomy of man and the world . . .

There is no longer any need for God as a working hypothesis, whether in morals, politics, or science.

Even if Bonhoeffer does not accept all the developments himself, he is prepared to concede these points to the person who is not a Christian, and he refuses to challenge any of these developments as being a rejection of Christian assumptions.

The attack by Christian apologetic upon the adulthood of the world I consider to be in the first place pointless, in the second ignoble, and in the third un-Christian. Pointless, because it looks to me like an attempt to put a grown-up man back into adolescence, *i.e.* to make him dependent on things on which he is not in fact dependent any more, thrusting him back into the midst of problems which are in fact not problems for him

any more. Ignoble, because this amounts to an effort to exploit the weakness of man for purposes alien to him and not freely subscribed to by him. Un-Christian, because for Christ himself is being substituted one particular stage in the religiousness of man.

Bonhoeffer's refusal to challenge the presuppositions of naturalistic man leads him to present the Christian God in this kind of way:

God allows himself to be edged out of the world and on to the cross. God is weak and powerless in the world, and that is exactly the way, the only way, in which he can be with us and help us. Matthew 8:17 makes it crystal clear that it is not by his omnipotence that Christ helps us, but by his weakness and suffering . . . Man's religiosity makes him look in his distress to the power of God in the world; he uses God as a *Deus ex machina*. The Bible however directs him to the powerlessness and suffering of God; only a suffering God can help.

To the person who does not already believe, however, this language must sound like the language of symbol; and it must seem like an invitation to make a leap of faith for which there are no compelling reasons.

There are right ways, and there are wrong

Dr C. E. M. Joad, who died in 1953, was the head of the Department of Philosophy, Birkbeck College, London.

and unkind ways in which to challenge the assumption of the autonomy of man. But if the Christian refuses at crucial points to say *NO*, he is likely to find that his gospel is transformed into something quite different.

▷ It is sometimes suggested that while most Christians are tolerant, it is the Biblical Christian who is the most intolerant. But it is only fair to point out that even those whose approach seems to be the most tolerant and all-inclusive feel the need to draw some lines and say 'we cannot have this'.

Emmanuel Amand de Mendieta:

We must become more and more 'intolerant' of the bigoted sectarian Catholic who is not an Evangelical, and of the bigoted and sectarian Evangelical who is not a Catholic ... On the other hand, the so-called 'moderate' Anglican, who is neither Catholic nor Evangelical, but prefers to follow a kind of practical middle way, which, for our souls' health, ought to be vigorously excluded, is even further from the Anglican vision.

▷ In serious discussion, disagreement and negation can contribute towards better understanding. We often suffer from an unjustified fear of controversy. Its ultimate objective is the truth and not mere negation.

Arnold Lunn:

The prevailing prejudice against controversy is partly due to our English distrust of logical argument and partly to a silly confusion which equates the quarrelsome with the controversial, silly because it is the inability to see another man's point of view which makes people quarrelsome, and the ability to understand the other man's position which makes a good controversialist.

▷ All the negatives in this context are intended to emphasize something very *positive*. *Peter*, for example, says:

By the name of Jesus Christ of Nazareth, whom you crucified, whom God raised from the dead, by him this man is standing before you well. This is the stone which was rejected by you builders, but which has become the head of the corner. And there is salvation in no one else, for there is no other name under heaven given among men by which we must be saved.

With some writers who claim to be positive in their approach, one is forced to wonder if they have ever really *felt* the profound despair and nihilism of many today:

John Wren-Lewis:

The thing that makes me angriest of all ... is when people seize joyfully upon the failures of the modern world as occasions for urging a return to the Christian faith, for the truth is that the real Christian faith is the very thing that could give and should give us the confidence to press on with our technological/humanist tasks in the belief that there is no limit to the possibility of success.

The approach of this book does not mean seizing joyfully upon the failures of the modern world. It means simply that one begins with a real sympathy with those who feel these failures most keenly; and then goes on to consider the alternatives.

Simplification distorts the truth and is bound to be superficial

▷ Some kind of simplification is demanded in almost every field:

Bronowski writing about the sciences:

What we try to reach ... is the simplest law, that will hold together the total complex of our evidence.

Norman Hampson writing about history:

As always, the historian must choose between generalizations which are never quite true in any specific instance and an incomprehensible anarchy of individual cases.

Aldous Huxley writing about some of the

dilemmas of the modern world in his Preface to *Brave New World Revisited*:

Life is short and information endless: nobody has time to do everything. In practice we are generally forced to choose between an unduly brief exposition and no exposition at all. Abbreviation is a necessary evil and the abbreviator's business is to make the best of a job which, though intrinsically bad, is still better than nothing. He must learn to simplify, but not to the point of falsification. He must learn to concentrate on the essentials of a situation, but without ignoring too many of the reality's qualifying side-issues. In this way he may be able to tell not indeed the whole truth (for the whole truth about almost any subject is incompatible with brevity), but considerably more than the dangerous quarter-truths and half-truths which have always been the current coin of thought.

▷ A sense of historical perspective will remind us that specialization and concentration on narrow fields has been forced on us comparatively recently. In the past men had few suspicions about the person whose knowledge covered many fields.

Norman Hampson writing about the outlook of the Enlightenment:

The Enlightenment was, to a remarkable degree, a period when the culture of the educated man was thought to take in the whole of human knowledge ... In dealing with an age which would have regarded the conception of 'two cultures' as equivalent to no culture at all, there is perhaps as much distortion in the specialist investigation of one subject in isolation from its contemporary context, as in the more superficial survey of the period as a whole. I certainly feel that whatever insight into the Enlightenment I have been able to attain is directly due to this kind of synthetic approach.

▷ Simplicity is not necessarily always a mark of naivety or ignorance. Socrates did much of his arguing with people in the market place.

▷ There is a good theological reason for simplicity:

Jesus said:

Truly, I say to you, whoever does not receive the kingdom of God like a child shall not enter it.

At that time Jesus declared, 'I thank thee, Father, Lord of heaven and earth, that thou hast hidden these things from the wise and understanding and revealed them to babes; yea, Father, for such was thy gracious will. All things have been delivered to me by my Father; and no one knows the Son except the Father, and no one knows the Father except the Son and any one to whom the Son chooses to reveal him. Come to me, all who labour and are heavy laden, and I will give you rest. Take my yoke upon you, and learn from me; for I am gentle and lowly in heart, and you will find rest for your souls. For my yoke is easy, and my burden is light.

Why the mania for consistency?

Aldous Huxley:

No man is by nature exclusively domiciled in one universe ... The only completely consistent people are the dead; the living are never anything but diverse. But such is man's pride, such is his intellectually vicious love of system and fixity, such is his terror and hatred of life, that the majority of human beings refuse to accept the facts. Men do not want to admit that they are what in fact they are – each one a colony of separate individuals, of whom now one and now another consciously lives with the life that animates the whole organism and directs its destinies. They want, in their pride and their terror, to be monsters of stiff consistency; they pretend, in the teeth of the facts, that they are one person all the time, thinking one set of thoughts, pursuing one course of action throughout life.

▷ The concern for consistency is simply part of a concern for the truth. If we give up the hope of being consistent, we give up hope of finding the truth. And Huxley's starting-point is a profound scepticism. (See further p. 59.) And it is perhaps not unfair to ask where this abandonment of any concern for consistency led him. By 1954, in his *Doors of Perception* he was advocating taking such drugs as mescalin in order to enjoy experiences which would reveal something of the truth of the universe. And towards the end of his life he was still advocating drugs as the only way to solve the problem of truth. (See p. 59.)

▷ Truth has to do with life, with the everyday

business of living, and not simply with rarified experiences. We have to live in the world as it is, and if our philosophy of life does not correspond with life as it is, life must become intolerable to a greater or lesser extent. The many extracts from *Alice in Wonderland* in this book are not included to raise a cheap laugh at the expense of others or to mock the weaknesses of others. They are included because they show vividly the difficulty of living in a world where there is no consistency, where people and things do not obey the usual laws.

John Lehmann:

Alice ... is the representative of common sense, in a world gone crazy. This world is inhabited by beings who put logic before sense and feeling, only the logic happens to be phoney, upside-down logic ... I call them nonsense-intellectuals. These beings – Humpty Dumpty, the March Hare, the Mad Hatter, the Queen of Hearts, the Gryphon, and the rest – are forever snubbing, contradicting, bossing Alice about quite callously, and proving that *they* know best by arguments which are nonsense but nevertheless satisfy *them*. Alice knows in her heart that they are wrong, but she cannot get the better of them in the argument game. Only at the end of Alice in Wonderland does Alice at last score in an argument; in the trial scene, where the King, who is conducting the trial, suddenly notices that Alice is growing larger and larger, and announces 'Rule forty-two. All persons more than a mile high to leave the court.' Alice immediately points out that, if the rule is the oldest in the book – as the King asserts that it is – then it ought to be rule number one. The King turns pale – and that is really the beginning of the end of the nonsense-intellectuals.

We must therefore make our own choice: if we abandon the search for consistency, we must accept the consequences.

Is there really any significant difference between the Biblical answer and the others?

The Biblical answer is not 'Scholastic' (compare Answer 2). To say that Christian beliefs are open to verification does not mean that certain beliefs can be proved by reason quite apart from God's revelation. It is not a question of laying down certain axioms and then showing that Christian beliefs must necessarily follow from these axioms. This is the Scholastic approach which lies behind the traditional arguments for the existence of God. To verify Christian beliefs means that we start with the *whole* system of Christian beliefs; we then test them by seeing how well they fit the facts.

It is not authoritarian (compare Answer 2). The Christian does not need to, and in fact he ought not to, speak from a position of authority. He should not say, 'This is the truth and you *must* accept it simply because I say so, or because the infallible Bible or the infallible Church says so.' There should be no suggestion of ' "Will you come into my parlour?" said the spider to the fly'. When the Christian is talking to the person who does not share his presuppositions, his challenge will take this form: 'I am not asking you to believe simply because someone is

telling you to believe. I want you to be convinced by yourself of your own free will. If you reject Christian beliefs, do your own beliefs fit the facts any better? You have to live, like anybody else; you have to eat and work, to love and die. You and I are both faced with the business of living. If this is what you believe, do you actually *live* in this way? Do you really live as if you believe these things to be true? Do your beliefs square with everything else that you know about yourself and about life? If you reach the point at which you realize that your beliefs do not fit the facts, then you may be prepared to think again and consider whether Christian beliefs fit the facts better.'

It is not Rationalistic (compare Answer 3). Verifying Christian beliefs does not mean that they must be tailored to fit the presuppositions of every man. Testing Christian beliefs in this way does not mean altering them, or watering them down to make them acceptable to the man who has already ruled God out of his thinking. There will always be the challenge to repentance and faith; but it will not be a blind or unthinking faith; for every man has the right to ask 'How can I know if this is true?' and to expect substantial answers. Repentance for the rationalist will mean reaching the point at which he realizes that he has been wrong, because his rationalism does not fit the facts, and decides to start with a new set of presuppositions – the Christian presuppositions.

It is not purely 'Existential' (compare Answer 5). Verifying Christian beliefs means that we cannot by-pass the question of whether they are true or not. We dare not say that we will stake our lives on these beliefs, regardless of whether or not they are objectively true. And we dare not simply believe them if our reason tells us that they are unconvincing or absurd. If we are convinced that these beliefs are true, and want to become Christians, we will need to take a *step of faith*; but it does not need to be, and ought not to be, a *leap of blind faith*. Becoming a Christian is not like throwing oneself off a cliff, not knowing whether one will land safely at the bottom. It is more like the process of finding out about another person and then knowing him personally and trusting him. Or it is like the process of learning to swim, knowing that, however strange the idea of floating in water may seem, countless other people have learned how to swim. Complete certainty will come *after* we have taken the step of faith; but we can be reasonably certain of the truth of Christianity even *before* we take the step.

It is not Mystical (compare Answer 6). We cannot hope to find out whether Christianity is true by switching off our minds and hoping to enjoy a mystical experience which will make everything clear to us. If we are convinced about Christian beliefs and take the step of faith, we will sooner or later *feel* its truth. But we cannot become Christians by trying to induce a mystical experience which by-passes our thinking processes.

WHERE DO WE GO FROM HERE?

If the question for you now is the evidence for the person of Jesus himself, the meaning of his death and evidence of his resurrection, turn to BOOK THREE.

If the questions are more basic, going back to our understanding of God, man and the universe, go on to BOOK TWO.

REFERENCES

PAGE 5
Lewis Carroll, *Alice in Wonderland*, Macmillan 1966, pp. 108; 110
Thomas Sherlock, *The Trial of the Witness of the Resurrection of Jesus*, London 1729; in Paul Hazard, *The European Mind 1680–1715*, Penguin 1964, pp. 96–97

PAGE 6
Bishop Butler, Advertisement to first edition of *The Analogy*; in Basil Willey, *The Eighteenth Century Background*, Chatto and Windus 1946, p. 82
J. S. Mill, *Autobiography*, World's Classics, p. 36
Nietzsche's Letter to his friend Von Gersdorff; in Colin Wilson, *The Outsider*, Pan 1967, p. 132
Mahatma Gandhi, Address on Christmas Day, 1931; in A. R. Vidler, *Objections to Christian Belief*, Pelican 1963, pp. 50–51
Colin Wilson, *Religion and the Rebel*, Gollancz 1957, p. 29

PAGE 7
James Mitchell, *The god I want*, Constable 1967, p. 2
C. E. M. Joad, *Is Christianity True?*, Eyre and Spottiswoode 1943, p. 14
Henri Barbusse, *L'Enfer*, tr. John Rodker, Joiner and Steele 1932, p. 9
Michael Harrington, *The Accidental Century*, Pelican 1967, p. 116
C. E. M. Joad, *Is Christianity True?*, p. 20
Margaret Cole, Essay in *What I Believe*, Allen and Unwin 1966, pp. 74–75

PAGE 12
Psalm 19: 1–4; Job 26: 8, 9, 14; Romans 1: 19, 20

PAGE 13
Richard Wurmbrand, *Tortured for Christ*, Hodder and Stoughton 1967, p. 23

PAGE 14
Romans 2: 1, 14–15; Exodus 33: 11; Amos 3: 7; Exodus 24: 3–4

PAGE 15
Jeremiah 1: 9–11; 36: 4; Psalm 119; Hebrews 1: 1; 2 Peter 1: 21; Matthew 5: 17–19; John 10: 34–36; 5: 39; Mark 12: 35–36; Matthew 19: 3–5; Luke 24: 44–45; John 14: 26; 16: 12–13

PAGE 16
1 Corinthians 2: 12–13; Galatians 1: 6–9; 2 Timothy 1: 13–14; Matthew 11: 27; John 14: 6–10

PAGE 17
John 1: 18; Hebrews 1: 1–2; Deuteronomy 29: 29; 1 Corinthians 13: 12; 2: 12–13; 14: 37; Genesis 15: 5–16

PAGE 18
Exodus 4: 1–9; 7: 17; 14: 4, 18; Deuteronomy 4: 9–14; 1 Kings 18: Deuteronomy 18: 18

PAGE 19
Isaiah 41: 20; 48: 3–5; Ezekiel 6: 7; John 6: 68; 2: 11; 20: 26–28; Acts 2: 22–36

PAGE 20
1 Corinthians 15: 3–8; Luke 1: 1–4

PAGE 21
J. Bronowski, *Science and Human Values*, Penguin 1964, pp. 33–34; 38–40; 66, 72
John Wren-Lewis, 'Does Science Destroy Christian Belief?' in *Fact, Faith and Fantasy*, Collins 1964, pp. 14; 20

PAGE 23
J. Bronowski, *Science and Human Values*, pp. 49; 52–53; 57
Aldous Huxley, *Do What You Will* (Essays), Watts and Co. 1937, p. 195

PAGE 24
Pieter Geyl, *Napoleon: For and Against*, Penguin 1965, pp. 15–18

PAGE 25
C. S. Lewis, *Surprised by Joy*, Collins Fontana 1959, pp. 178–179

PAGE 26
Frank Morison, *Who Moved the Stone?*, Faber, pp. 11–12

N. P. Williams (and W. Sanday), *Form and Content in the Christian Tradition*, 1916; in A. R. Vidler, *Twentieth Century Defenders of the Faith*, SCM Press 1965, p. 90
C. E. M. Joad, *Is Christianity True?* p. 97
C. E. M. Joad, *The Book of Joad*, Faber and Faber 1944, p. 213
Bertrand Russell, *The Problems of Philosophy*, Home University Library 1967, pp. 9–10
Alasdair MacIntyre, *Difficulties in Christian Belief*, SCM Press 1959, p. 31

PAGE 28
Bertrand Russell, *Human Knowledge: Its Scope and Limitations*, Allen and Unwin 1948, p. 448; 148
C. E. M. Joad, *The Recovery of Belief*, Faber and Faber 1952 pp. 13–14; 16; 46; 63

PAGE 29
Psalm 34: 8; 50: 14–15; Malachi 3: 10

PAGE 30
Matthew 11: 28–30; Psalm 34: 4; 116: 1–2; John 6: 66–69; 1: 14–16; 20: 27–28; 1 John 1: 1–4

PAGE 31
Thomas Aquinas, *Summa Theologica*, 1, Question 1; in *Historical Selections in the Philosophy of Religion*, ed. Ninian Smart, SCM Press 1962, p. 62

PAGE 32
H. Denzinger, *Enchiridion Symbolorum* (Documents of the First Vatican Council); in C. Brown, *Philosophy and the Christian Faith*, Tyndale Press 1969, p. 163
Cardinal J. C. Heenan, *Our Faith*, Nelson 1956, pp. 82–83

PAGES 33, 34
The Koran, tr. N. J. Dawood, Penguin 1964, Sura 29: 50, p. 195; 2: 2–4, 23–24, pp. 324–325; 13: 27–28, p. 142; 42: 35, p. 153; 3: 2–3, p. 395; 46: 7–9, p. 124; 7: 203–204, p. 256; 3: 7–8, p. 395

PAGE 35
J. Bronowski, *Science and Human Values*, p. 44
Francis Bacon, *Novum Organum*, 1: LXV; in Basil Willey, *The Seventeenth Century Background*, p. 32
Francis Bacon, *De augmentis*, IX; in Willey, *The Seventeenth Century Background*, pp. 32–33
Thomas Browne, *Religio medici*, 1: X; 1: XLVIII; in Willey, *The Seventeenth Century Background*, p. 59
John Locke, *An Essay Concerning Human Understanding*, 4: XVIII: 2
Basil Willey, *The Seventeenth Century Background*, pp. 33–34

PAGE 36
Lord Herbert of Cherbury, *De la Vérité*, pp. 51f.; in Willey, *The Seventeenth Century Background*, p. 114
In Willey, *The Seventeenth Century Background*, pp. 118–120
Essay, 'What is Dogma?'; in A. R. Vidler, *Twentieth Century Defenders of the Faith*, pp. 51–53

PAGE 37
H. J. Blackham, *Objections to Humanism*, Penguin 1963, p. 28
George Harrison, interview in *Melody Maker*, 16 December 1967
Dostoievsky, *The Brothers Karamazov*, Penguin, Vol. 1, pp. 288–311

PAGE 38
Emil Brunner, *The Christian Doctrine of Creation and Redemption*, Lutterworth 1952, pp. 240–241
'Don't Crush the Little Faith I Have', anonymous article in *Eternity*, 1965

PAGE 39
W. Cantwell Smith, *Questions of Religious Truth*, Gollancz 1967, pp. 48–49

PAGE 40
Ernst Cassirer, *The Renaissance Philosophy of Man*, University of Chicago Press 1948, pp. 10–11
Paul Hazard, *The European Mind 1680–1715*, pp. 8–9

PAGE 41
Paul Hazard, *The European Mind 1680–1715*, pp. 159–160; 499–502
René Descartes, *Everyman Discourse* 15 (three quotations)

PAGE 42
John Locke, *An Essay concerning Human Understanding*, 2: IX: 1; in Willey, *The Seventeenth Century Background*, p. 259; John Locke, 4: I: 1; 4: XVIII: 2
John Locke, in Willey, *The Eighteenth Century Background*, p. 32
John Locke, *An Essay concerning Human Understanding*, 4: XIX: 4
Paul Hazard, *The European Mind 1680–1715*, pp. 278, 282–283
G. R. Cragg, *The Church and the Age of Reason (1648–1789)*, Pelican 1960, p. 75

PAGE 43
Norman Hampson, *The Enlightenment*, Pelican 1968, pp. 186–187
Basil Willey, *The Eighteenth Century Background*, p. 107
J. Bronowski and Bruce Mazlish, *The Western Intellectual Tradition*, Penguin 1963, p. 330
S. T. Coleridge, *Biographia Literaria*; in Basil Willey, *Nineteenth Century Studies*, Chatto and Windus 1949, p. 43

PAGE 44
James Thurber, Essay in *What I Believe*, p. 138
H. J. Blackham, *Objections to Humanism*, p. 11
H. J. Blackham in *Prism*, October 1963
G. R. Cragg, *The Church and the Age of Reason*, Hodder and Stoughton 1962, p. 76
G. R. Cragg, *Reason and Authority in the Eighteenth Century*, CUP 1964

PAGE 45
Mark Pattison; in G. R. Cragg, *The Church and the Age of Reason*, p. 76
Basil Willey, *The Seventeenth Century Background*, p. 73
Basil Willey, *The Eighteenth Century Background*, p. 83
D. F. Strauss, *Life of Jesus*, tr. Marian Evans, 1846, Vol. 1, p. 71; (two quotations)

PAGE 46
Basil Willey, *The Eighteenth Century Background*, p. 237
Paul Hazard, *The European Mind 1680–1715*, pp. 139; 274
Thomas Carlyle; in Basil Willey, *Nineteenth Century Studies*, pp. 120–122

PAGE 47
A. J. Ayer, Essay in *What I Believe*, p. 14
Aldous Huxley, *Do What You Will* (Essays), pp. 2–3; 218–219; 234–235

PAGE 48
Jacquetta Hawkes, in *What I Believe*, p. 137
Rebecca West, in *What I Believe*, p. 176
Albert Einstein, in *What I Believe*, p. 27
Barbara Wooton, in *What I Believe*, p. 205
H. J. Blackham, *Objections to Humanism*, p. 13
David Hume, *Treatise of Human Nature*, 1: II: 6; in Basil Willey, *The Eighteenth Century Background*, p. 113
David Hume, *Treatise of Human Nature*, 1: III: 12
David Hume, *An Abstract of a Treatise of Human Nature;* in Bronowski and Mazlish, *Western Intellectual Tradition*, p. 528

PAGE 49
In Reardon, *Religious Thought in the Nineteenth Century*, CUP 1946, Introduction to Chapter on Kant

PAGE 50
W. Cantwell Smith, *Questions of Religious Truth*, p. 74
Radhakrishnan, *The Hindu View of Life*, London 1931, p. 38
K. M. Sen, *Hinduism*, Penguin 1969, p. 37
Christmas Humphreys, *Buddhism*, Penguin, p. 122
Leopold Sédar Senghor, on *African Socialism*, tr. Mercer Cook, Praeger 1964, pp. 41; 123

PAGE 51
J. Bronowski, *The Identity of Man*, Penguin 1965, p. 62
Aldous Huxley, *Do What You Will* (Essays), pp. 31, 37
Paul Tillich, 'On the Boundary Line', *Christian Century*, 6 December 1960, pp. 1435–1436
Teilhard de Chardin
John Robinson, *Exploration into God*, SCM Press 1967, pp. 139–141
W. Cantwell Smith, *Questions of Religious Truth*, pp. 57; 34–35; 37

PAGE 52
Alasdair MacIntyre, *Difficulties in Christian Belief*, SCM Press, p. 27
Lewis Carroll, *Alice in Wonderland*, pp. 88–89; 165; 180–181

PAGE 53
Voltaire; in Norman Hampson, *The Enlightenment*, p. 76
Hannah Arend, *The Human Condition*, University of Chicago 1969, p. 252

Colin Wilson, *The Outsider*, pp. 23–24
Michael Harrington, *The Accidental Century*, p. 45
J. Bronowski, *Science and Human Values*, p. 50

PAGE 54
David Hume, *Treatise of Human Nature*, 1: IV: 2; 1: IV: 7
Maurice Friedman, *To Deny Our Nothingness*, Gollancz 1967, pp. 223–224
C. E. M. Joad, *The Book of Joad*, p. 103
Time, 26 April 1968

PAGE 55
Harold Pinter, Programme Note for Royal Court Production of *The Room* and *The Dumb Waiter*; in John Russell Taylor, *Anger and After*, Penguin 1963, pp. 300–301
Eric Rhode, 'Poor Cow', *Listener*, 14 December 1967, p. 769
Simon Hoggart, *Guardian Weekly*, 26 December 1968
J. Bronowski, *Science and Human Values*, pp. 36–37
J. Wren-Lewis, *Fact, Faith and Fantasy*, p. 24

PAGE 56
Douglas Spanner in *The Church of England Newspaper*, 31 March 1967
C. S. Lewis, *Miracles*, Fontana 1960, p. 110
G. J. Warnock, *English Philosophy since 1900*; in Leslie Paul, *Alternatives to Christian Belief*, Hodder and Stoughton 1967, p. 139
Leslie Paul, *Alternatives to Christian Belief*, pp. 150–151

PAGE 57
George Eliot, *Letters* (1862); in Basil Willey, *Nineteenth Century Studies*, p. 249
Lessing, *Nathan the Wise*, Act III, Scene 7; Summary from C. Brown, *Philosophy and the Christian Faith*, p. 89
William James, *Pragmatism, A New Way for Some Old Ways of Thinking*, 1907; in C. Brown, *Philosophy and the Christian Faith*, p. 146
Thomas Arnold, *Introductory Lectures on Modern History* (1842); in Basil Willey *Nineteenth Century Studies*, p. 71
J. B. Priestley in *Literature and Western Man*; quoted by Calder-Marshall in *What I Believe*, p. 68
André Gide, *The God that Failed*, p. 198
George Orwell, *1984*, Penguin 1968, p. 220
Arthur Koestler, *The Ghost in the Machine*, Hutchinson 1967, p. 262

PAGE 58
Ignazio Silone, *The God that Failed*, p. 109
Nikita Struve, *Christians in Contemporary Russia*, Collins 1967, p. 288
Lewis Carroll, *Alice in Wonderland*, p. 124

PAGE 59
John Lehmann, 'Alice at the Sorbonne', *Listener*, 22 September 1966
Aldous Huxley, *Doors of Perception and Heaven and Hell*, Penguin 1969, pp. 23–25

PAGE 60
Emil Brunner, *The Christian Doctrine of Creation and Redemption*, p. 27

PAGE 61
Paul Tillich, *Shaking of the Foundations*, Penguin 1962, pp. 163–164
Paul Tillich, *The Courage to Be*, Fontana 1962, p. 185
Rudolph Bultmann, *Kerygma and Myth*, ed. H. W. Bartsch, SPCK 1953, p. 26; 1: X
W. Cantwell Smith, *Questions of Religious Truth*, pp. 68–69
T. de Chardin, *The Phenomenon of Man*, Fontana 1966, pp. 252; 256–257
John Robinson, *Honest to God*, SCM Press 1963, pp. 48–49

PAGE 62
John Robinson, *Exploration into God*, SCM Press 1967, p. 68 (two quotations)
Alan Richardson, *Science and Existence*, SCM Press 1957
Rosemary Haughton in *What I Believe*, p. 114
Leslie Paul, *Alternatives to Christian Belief*, pp. 204–205
The New Dutch Catechism, Burns and Oates 1967, pp. 261–262, 269

PAGE 63
Blaise Pascal, *Pensées*, tr. Martin Turnell, Harvill Press 1962, p. 163

PAGE 64
Bronowski and Mazlish, *The Western Intellectual Tradition*, pp. 276; 278
S. Kierkegaard, *Journals* (1854); in H. Diem, *Kierkegaard's Theology of Existence*, Oliver and Boyd 1959, p. 202
S. Kierkegaard, *Journals*, selected and tr. Alexander Dru, Fontana 1958, p. 44

PAGE 65
S. Kierkegaard, in Diem, *Kierkegaard's Theology of Existence*, p. 49
S. Kierkegaard, *Philosophical Fragments*, tr. David F. Swenson, Oxford and New York 1936, p. 87
Title page of S. Kierkegaard, *Philosophical Fragments*, Princeton 1957 edition
S. Kierkegaard, *Concluding Unscientific Postscript*, Princeton 1944, pp. 500; 503
S. Kierkegaard: in Diem, *Kierkegaard's Theology of Existence*, p. 49
S. Kierkegaard, *Philosophical Fragments*, pp. 358–359
S. Kierkegaard, *Journals*, ed. A. Dru, pp. 185–186
S. Kierkegaard, *The Last Years: Journals 1853–1855*, ed. and tr. Ronald Gregor Smith, Collins 1965, pp. 99–100
Herbert Read, Review of the above in *The Listener*

PAGE 66
H. J. Blackham, *Six Existential Thinkers*, Routledge and Kegan Paul 1965, p. 4
Karl Barth, *God, Grace and Gospel;* in T. F. Torrance, *Karl Barth, An Introduction to his Early Theology*, SCM Press 1962, p. 38

PAGE 67
T. F. Torrance, *Karl Barth*, pp. 49; 44–45; 143

PAGE 68
T. F. Torrance, *Karl Barth*, pp. 82; 44; 120–121

PAGE 69
T. F. Torrance, *Karl Barth*, pp. 87; 148
Karl Barth, *Anselm: Fides Quaerens Intellectum*, SCM Press 1960, pp. 69; 161; 71; 11
Karl Barth, *The Doctrine of the Word of God, Church Dogmatics*, 1 : 1, p. 31
T. F. Torrance, *Karl Barth*, pp. 164; 87

PAGE 70
T. F. Torrance, *Karl Barth*, p. 111
Stephen Neill, *The Interpretation of the New Testament 1861–1961*, Oxford 1964, p. 208 footnote
William Warren Bartley, *The Retreat to Commitment*, Chatto and Windus 1964, pp. 63; 219
C. E. M. Joad, *Is Christianity True?*, p. 20

PAGE 71
Beatrice Webb in *What I Believe*, p. 162
Colin Wilson, *Religion and the Rebel*, pp. 138–139
Lewis Carroll, *Alice in Wonderland*, pp. 220–221

PAGE 72
T. W. Fowle, *Nineteenth Century Opinion*, ed. Michael Goodwin, Pelican 1951, p. 117

PAGE 73
Colin Wilson, *The Outsider*, p. 224
Marghanita Laski, 'God and the Universe', *Week-End Telegraph*, 16 December 1966
Bartley, *The Retreat to Commitment*, pp. 35–36
Leslie Newbiggin, *Honest Religion for Secular Man*, SCM Press 1966, p. 10
J. S. Bezzant in *Objections to Christian Belief*, p. 78
T. J. J. Altizer and W. Hamilton, *Radical Theology and the Death of God*, 1966, p. 135
Ninian Smart, *World Religions: A Dialogue*, Penguin 1966, p. 88
Lewis Carroll, *Alice in Wonderland*, p. 206

PAGE 74
David Knowles, *What is Mysticism?*, Burns and Oates 1967
F. C. Happold, *Religious Faith and Twentieth Century Man*, Penguin 1966, pp. 172; 106
H. R. Rookmaaker, *Modern Art and the Death of a Culture*, IVP 1970, p. 202

PAGE 75
Albert Ayler, in J. Marks, *Rock and other Four Letter Words*, Bantam 1968; also Brian Wilson in the same
From BBC TV *Man Alive* programme 'Eastern Promise', 31 May 1972
Aldous Huxley, *Ends and Means*, Chatto and Windus 1937, p. 286
Brian Wilson, Larry Ramos and Peter Townsend in *Rock and other Four Letter Words*

PAGE 76
Christmas Humphreys, *Buddhism*, Penguin, pp. 180, 185–186
Dionysius the Areopagite, *The Mystical Theology*, Shrine of Wisdom Press; in Happold, *Religious Faith and Twentieth Century Man*, p. 112
Aldous Huxley, *Ends and Means*, pp. 289–290

PAGE 77
Nicholas of Cusa, *The Vision of God*, tr. E. G. Salter; in Happold, *Religious Faith and Twentieth Century Man*, p. 45
Simone Weil, article in *Theology*
F. C. Happold, *Religious Faith and Twentieth Century Man*, pp. 51–52; 149; 152

PAGE 78
F. C. Happold, *Religious Faith and Twentieth Century Man*, pp. 124; 68
C. E. M. Joad, *The Book of Joad*, pp. 72–73
F. C. Happold, p. 172
C. E. M. Joad, *Recovery of Belief*, Faber and Faber 1952, pp. 97–98

PAGE 79
Renan; in G. Galloway, *Philosophy of Religion*, International Theological Library
S. T. Coleridge, *Aids to Reflection*; in Basil Willey, *Nineteenth Century Studies*, p. 49
Ronald Knox, *Letter to Lady Acton*, 1956; in Evelyn Waugh, *Ronald Knox*, Fontana 1962, pp. 283–284

PAGE 80
H. E. Root, 'What is the Gospel?' *Theology*, June 1963
A. R. Vidler, Review of Clyde S. Kilby, *The Christian World of C. S. Lewis* in *Book Week*
Review in *Honey*, January 1967
Constance Padwick, *Temple Gairdner of Cairo*, SPCK 1929; pp. 148–149; 158

PAGE 81
Emil Brunner, *The Christian Doctrine of Creation and Redemption*

PAGE 82
Freud, *New Introductory Lectures on Psycho-Analysis*
Leslie Paul, *Alternatives to Christian Belief*, pp. 133–134
Colin Wilson, *Religion and the Rebel*, p. 177
Ann Jellico, Interview in *New Theatre Magazine*; in John Russell Taylor, *Anger and After*, pp. 69–70

PAGE 83
Colin Wilson, *The Outsider*, p. 296

PAGE 84
John Habgood, *Religion and Science*, Mills and Boon 1964, pp. 141–142
New Dutch Catechism, pp. 236–237

PAGE 85
John 6: 68–69; 16: 29–30
G. E. Lessing, *Eine Duplik*; in Paul Hazard, *European Thought in the Eighteenth Century*, p. 495
Psalm 119: 34; 119: 18

PAGE 86
2 Peter 1: 5–6; 1 Corinthians 14: 20; Colossians 1: 9; 1 Peter 3: 15
Dietrich Bonhoeffer, *Letters and Papers from Prison*, Fontana 1959, p. 189

PAGE 87
Bonhoeffer, *Letters and Papers from Prison*, pp. 146–147; 164

PAGE 88
Emmanuel Amand de Mendieta, Essay in *The Anglican Synthesis* ed. W. R. F. Browning, Peter Smith 1964, pp. 155–156
Arnold Lunn and C. E. M. Joad, *Is Christianity True?*, p. 310
Acts 4: 10–12
John Wren-Lewis, in *What I Believe*, p. 235
J. Bronowski, *The Identity of Man*, p. 45
Norman Hampson, *The Enlightenment*, p. 129

PAGE 89
Aldous Huxley, *Brave New World Revisited*, Introduction
Norman Hampson, *The Enlightenment*, p. 11
Mark 10: 15; Matthew 11: 25–30
Aldous Huxley, *Do What You Will* (Essays), pp. 185–186

PAGE 90
John Lehmann, 'Alice at the Sorbonne', pp. 424f.

INDEX